ORRIBLE BRITISH TRUE CRIME

VOLUME TWO

Ben Oakley

TITLES BY BEN OAKLEY

FICTION

HARRISON LAKE INVESTIGATIONS
The Camden Killer
The Limehouse Hotel
Monster of the Algarve

HONEYSUCKLE GOODWILLIES
The Mystery of Grimlow Forest
The Mystery of Crowstones Island

SUBNET SF TRILOGY
Unknown Origin
Alien Network
Final Contact

NONFICTION

TRUE CRIME
Bizarre True Crime Series
Orrible British True Crime Series
The Monstrous Book of Serial Killers
True Crime 365 series
Year of the Serial Killer

OTHER NONFICTION
The Immortal Hour: The True Story of Netta Fornario
Suicide Prevention Handbook

Look for more in the Orrible British True Crime Series!

OUT NOW!

Copyright © 2022 Ben Oakley.

First published in 2022 by Twelvetrees Camden.

This edition 2022.

The right of Ben Oakley to be identified as the
Author of the Work has been asserted by him in accordance
with the Copyright, Designs and Patents Act 1988.

Visit the author's website at www.benoakley.co.uk

All rights reserved. No part of this book may be reproduced, or stored in a
retrieval system, or transmitted in any form or by any means, electronic,
mechanical, photocopying, recording, or otherwise, without express
written permission of the publisher.

Each case has been fully researched and fact-checked to bring you the
best stories possible and all information is correct at the time of
publication. This book is meant for entertainment and informational
purposes only.

While the publisher and author have used their best efforts in preparing
this book, they make no representations or warranties with respect to the
accuracy or completeness of the contents of this book. Neither the
publisher nor the author shall be liable for any loss of profit or any other
commercial damages, including but not limited to special, incidental,
consequential, personal, or other damages.

The author or publisher cannot be held responsible for any errors or
misinterpretation of the facts detailed within. The book is not intended to
hurt or defame individuals or companies involved.

ISBN: 978-1-7397149-2-5

Cover design by Ben Oakley.

For information about special discounts available
for bulk purchases, sales promotions, book signings,
trade shows, and distribution, contact
sales@twelvetreescamden.com

Twelvetrees Camden Ltd
71-75 Shelton Street, Covent Garden
London, WC2H 9JQ

www.twelvetreescamden.com

Orrible British True Crime Volume 2

The Beenham Murders 11

Largest Cash Robbery in UK History 23

The Blackout Killer 35

Burning of Mary Channing 49

Peter Tobin & Bible John 57

Notting Hill Murder of Vera Page 69

The Bikini Bloodbath Murder 79

Charles Walton and the Quinton Witch 89

The MI6 Catfishing Case 99

Madness of the Eriksson Twins 109

Reincarnation of Two Murdered Girls 117

Smelly Bobby Tulip 125

Mystery of the Body in the Tree 135

Visions of Murder 143

Killings of Templeton Woods 149

From the 18th Century to the 21st, a bonanza collection of 15 short British true crime stories covering murder, witchcraft, robbery, serial killers, and a body in a tree!

1. The Beenham Murders

A child killer claimed two young lives, shocking a small Berkshire village, but the killer was a local who had already claimed another victim six months earlier, and would escape justice for 45 years.

2. Largest Cash Robbery in UK History

What do a car salesman, a garage owner, a roofer, a doorman, an insider, a company director and two MMA fighters have in common? Together, they pulled off the largest cash robbery in UK history.

3. The Blackout Killer

During wartime London, as the German bombs were raining down, a serial killer was at work who brought a new kind of darkness to the cold and lonely streets of the British Capital.

4. Burning of Mary Channing

A young woman obsessed with free money, parties, and multiple lovers, poisoned her husband and was burned at the stake for her troubles in front of thousands of people.

5. Peter Tobin & Bible John

Three murders in the late 1960s linked to the mysterious Bible John remain unsolved to this day, with a strong suspicion that serial killer Peter Tobin was the man behind the unidentified murderer.

6. Notting Hill Murder of Vera Page

A ten-year-old girl was abducted and murdered in Notting Hill, leading to a 100-year-old cold case, which despite a strong suspect and solid investigatory work, remains officially unsolved to this day.

7. The Bikini Bloodbath Murder

On the hottest day of the century, a woman sunbathing in her bikini had her throat cut by an unidentified attacker, then left in a pool of blood for her husband to find.

8. Charles Walton and the Quinton Witch

In 1945 Britain, witchcraft was long gone, but ask any local from the sleepy town of Lower Quinton, what happened to Charles Walton, and they'll tell you it was witchcraft!

9. The MI6 Catfishing Case

A teenager created multiple online identities to trick his friend into believing he had been recruited by an MI6 agent to kill him, thereby setting up his own murder, in a bizarre tale of catfishing.

10. Madness of the Eriksson Twins

Two Swedish sisters said to be experiencing a shared psychosis called folie à deux went on days of bizarre and dangerous behaviour in England before ultimately ending with murder.

11. Reincarnation of Two Murdered Girls

A year after two sisters were killed in a hit-and-run, their parents gave birth to twin girls, and claimed they were the reincarnated souls of the sisters, in one of the most convincing cases of reincarnation.

12. Smelly Bobby Tulip

Robert Black was convicted of four murders but has been linked to at least 21 more, making him one of Britain's most prolific serial killers, with an unusual and disturbing taste for young girls.

13. Mystery of the Body in the Tree

In 1940s England, a group of young boys were playing in the forest when they found a dead woman stuffed into the middle of a wych elm tree.

14. Visions of Murder

From a brutal murder in London to one of the most convincing cases of psychic mediumship in the history of true crime.

15. Killings of Templeton Woods

After the first Templeton Woods murder, girls stopped walking the streets alone, after the second, the area became ground zero for Britain's most infamous cold case, with links to the Zodiac Killer.

The Beenham Murders

A child killer claimed two young lives, shocking a small Berkshire village, but the killer was a local who had already claimed another victim six months earlier, and would escape justice for 45 years.

1960's Britain was infamous for a number of child killers, not least the Moors Murderers and the Cannock Chase Monster, but there was another who was convicted of two murders and were it not for the hard work of cold case investigators, would have got away with a third.

The small village of Beenham in Berkshire traces its roots to the 12th Century when it became a Church of England Parish, with Saint Mary's church being the focal point of the community. Jump forward 900 years and the population of the village remains below 500.

Over a six month period from 1966 to 1967, three murders took place that shocked not only the community but the entire nation. It focussed attention on Beenham in such a way that the village has never really escaped the shadow of what became known as the Beenham Murders.

The killer, David Burgess, was caught just weeks after the last murder and was convicted in 1967 for the murder of two nine-year-old girls – two of the three Beenham victims. The other victim, six months earlier, was a 17-year-old who was not connected to Burgess at the time.

It was 45 years later in 2011 when the 17-year-old victim was connected to him. When interviewed by police accusing him of the murder, he calmly looked up from the interview table, smiled, and said '*prove it.*'

Oakwood Farm

At the tail-end of a cold October in 1966, 17-year-old Kent-born Yolande Waddington took a job as a nanny with the Jagger family in Beenham. The location was accessible as Yolande lived with her parents only nine miles away in nearby Newbury.

Yolande's vocation in life was to become a children's nurse and nannying was one of the routes to take in the 1960s, experience over education tended to bring social jobs within easier reach. The Jagger family ran Oakwood

Farm and needed assistance with their children, and Yolande was the perfect choice.

Becoming a live-in nanny at a young age, though Yolande's dream, tended to cut them off from their own social circles. So it was met with delight from the Jagger family that Yolande's own family was only a few miles away.

On 28th October 1966, after only three days of working with the Jagger's, Yolande would meet an untimely demise. She spent the evening writing a letter to her boyfriend then shortly after 10pm, when the children were asleep, she walked away from the farm and down the road to the post box, 15 minutes away.

At 10.35pm, she jumped into the Six Bells pub, a local drinking haven, and bought some cigarettes. It was the last time anyone saw her alive – apart from her killer. The following morning, when the Jagger parents found their live-in nanny had not returned from the night before, they became concerned.

They phoned Yolande's boyfriend who said he hadn't heard from her and had no idea where she was. Shortly before noon on the 29th, the Jagger's phoned the police and a search got underway. Less than 24 hours after that, and a day before Halloween, Beenham was about to be scarred by its first of three brutal murders.

Cow shed discovery

After an intensive search of the village and surrounding fields, and in the late morning of the 30th, two farm workers traipsed into a cow shed on the outskirts of the village and made a macabre discovery. Beside some bales of hay, they found bloodstained items of clothing.

Realising the clothes may have belonged to the missing girl, they searched around the shed and just a short distance away in a nearby ditch, they found the brutalised body of Yolande. A large scale murder investigation was launched that at the time was the largest Berkshire had ever seen.

Yolande was found half-nude and had been tied at the wrists by baling twine, a hemp-like thin rope that's used to tie hay bales together. An autopsy showed that she had been strangled to death with the same cord, stabbed twice in the chest, and left for dead within an hour of leaving the pub.

Unusually, the stab wounds were only two inches deep and it appeared the killer had stabbed her with a small penknife merely to subdue her before killing by strangulation. It was unusual as most murders by knife are carried out with much larger blades.

Detectives were shipped in from across the county along with some officers from Scotland Yard. A search of the area was carried out by them and United States Airmen who were based at

USAF Greenham Common – now RAF Greenham – just ten miles away from Beenham.

Within a day of the murder, a broken blade belonging to a pen knife was found a few hundred metres from the cow shed and it had remnants of blood on it. Testing of the blood on the blade and on her clothing uncovered two different blood groups, one belonging to Yolande, the other to the killer.

The local police stepped up their investigation and interviewed approximately 4,000 people, including everyone from the village and many from the surrounding areas. In the days before DNA testing, blood testing and fingerprints were one of the primary forensic methods.

To that effect, the police set up the first mass blood testing drive in UK investigation history. They set up a testing centre and requested that every adult male from the age of 16 in and around the village of Beenham had to give a sample of their blood.

A new horror

By early November 1966, just two weeks after the murder, over 200 blood samples had been submitted and tested by forensic scientists. Four men were found to have the same blood type as the blood at the scene but due to various alibis and other evidence, were discounted as suspects.

One suspect, who would one day come back to haunt the investigation, was 19-year-old David Burgess. He had been in the pub when Yolande had come in for cigarettes and was known to have had around 14 pints of beer.

He claimed that he left the pub shortly after Yolande but saw her walk away and nothing else. His blood type didn't exactly match, with only three of the four testing aspects coming up as positive.

For that reason, Burgess was removed from the suspect list, and it would be 45 years before the truth came out.

By early 1967, the investigation had started to run on empty. With no new evidence or suspects to look at, the case went cold but it never closed. Then, as the horrors of Yolande's mysterious murder began to pass into the realm of the unsolved, a new horror was awaiting Beenham.

On 17th April 1967, shortly after the bell rang signalling the end of the school day, two nine-year-old school friends, Jeanette Wigmore and Jacqueline Williams, jumped on their bicycles and began the short ride home.

They went to Jeanette's home, where her father, Tony, saw the two girls playing near the lane at the back of the house. It was the last time they were ever seen alive.

Blake's Pit

By 6:45pm when dinner was waiting on the table and Jeanette hadn't come in from the cool Spring evening, her father went to Jacqueline's family home to look for her. When both families realised the girls were missing, they informed other locals who put together a search party.

Remembering that Jeanette liked to play at a local gravel pit called Blake's Pit opposite a quarry site called Fisher's gravel pits, Tony drove there ahead of other searchers and parked up. At 8.30pm, he found both bicycles lying flat on the ground. A short distance away, he discovered the body of his daughter, face down in water at the bottom of a bank.

When the local search party descended on Blake's Pit, they found Jacqueline's body just 100 metres away from Jeanette's, also face down in water and hurriedly covered with leaves and twigs. The time of death of both girls was in the hour before dinner was served at the Wigmore household.

Once again, Beenham was home to cold-blooded murder. Autopsies showed that Jeanette had been stabbed five times in the chest and throat, while Jacqueline was sexually assaulted and strangled by the killer's bare hands before being drowned in a small pool of water.

For the second time in six months, Scotland Yard sent a team of officers and another 80 or so specially trained police to Beenham. The entirety of the gravel pit and the waters were drained by specialist teams looking for the murder weapon which was never found.

The investigation involved the entire village and surrounding areas where almost 1,500 statements were taken and hundreds more interviews carried out. Fear had taken hold of Beenham and many residents took their children out of school until the killer was caught.

The rabbit hunter

It seemed to be no coincidence that the murder of Yolande and the two school friends were so close together, and many villagers were confident it was the same culprit behind them. The police continued their investigation of the gravel pit and attempted to create a timeline of the entire village from the statements that had been provided.

They discovered that two local brothers were working at the quarry at the time and brought them in for questioning. John Burgess said that he and the last of his colleagues had left Fishers gravel pits at around 6pm but his brother, dumper driver David Burgess, had gone to Blake's Pit to check some of his rabbit-snares as he was a rabbit hunter in his spare time.

Beenham-born Burgess had returned 20 minutes later and waited with some of the other workers before making their own way home. He was asked to hand over the clothing he was wearing that day to police but told them it already looked bad as he was near the area anyway.

Realising that Burgess had already been a suspect in Yolande's murder six months earlier, they doubled-down on him as the killer but needed proof. Fortunately for the two girl's families, evidence was easy to come by.

Jeannette's blood type was AB/MN, one of the rarest kinds. It was matched to unwashed blood splatter on a boot which Burgess had been wearing at work the day of the murder. With a blood match and the statement from his brother, Burgess was arrested and charged with the two girl's murders on 7th May 1967.

In less than 20 minutes, he had taken the lives of two girls playing happily in the shadow of their hometown. Just three days before his arrest and two weeks after the murders, Burgess was seen buying drinks for Jacqueline's father – knowing he had killed his daughter.

Confession

At his trial, Burgess came up with a story of witnessing an unidentified man standing over the body of one of the girls. The man, who he referred to as McNab, threatened him and his family with severe consequences should he say anything about what he had seen.

Unsurprisingly, the jury didn't believe him and found him guilty of both murders. He was given two life sentences and condemned to rot in jail for 29 years. As much as the police wanted to pin Yolande's murder on him, they simply didn't have the evidence needed and so her case went cold.

In May 1996, after 29 years in prison, Burgess was released on license but couldn't keep out of trouble. He failed to report back to prison and got involved in drunken behaviour. Then, in early 1998, he carried out an armed robbery on a bank in Havant, Hampshire, before being arrested in nearby Portsmouth. He was convicted and sentenced to another 10 years.

While in prison for the second time, he confessed to Yolande's murder but told the prison officers and subsequent investigating officers to '*prove it*'. While serving his time for armed robbery, he was given additional sentences for wounding another prisoner with intent back in 1978 and making false statements to receive benefits in 1996.

Justice finds a way

It seemed the police were wanting a way to keep him where they could watch him as they attempted to prove he had killed Yolande, and in 2010, the case was reopened. Using new DNA testing techniques, investigators discovered DNA on Yolande's clothes that matched Burgess's.

In early 2012, the then 64-year-old Burgess was convicted of her murder and sentenced to an additional 27 years in prison. 45 years after her death, Yolande and her family finally got the justice they deserved.

Police learned that he had followed Yolande from the Six Bell's pub before deciding to sexually assault her and killed her so she could never speak out against him. Jeanette and Jacqueline playing in the gravel pit were opportunistic murders that were carried out with no emotion or humanity.

For Beenham, their 1,000-year history would be forever tainted by the horrors of one of their own, a child killer who was no more than a child himself, hiding in plain sight.

Fortunately, Yolande's voice was finally heard, 45 years after her death, with the help of modern forensic technology, proving that justice will always find a way, and that criminals of any age will always be looking over their shoulder, waiting for the past to catch up.

Largest Cash Robbery in UK History

What do a car salesman, a garage owner, a roofer, a doorman, an insider, a company director and two MMA fighters have in common? Together, they pulled off the largest cash robbery in UK history.

On 21st February 2006, armed with assault rifles and submachine guns, a well-organised gang stormed the Securitas depot in Tonbridge, Kent. A few hours later, in the early hours of the 22nd, they made off with £53million in cash – more money than they knew what to do with.

By 2008, 36 people had been arrested in relation to the robbery, including the eight main criminals who would go on to be sentenced for it. By the end of 2008, and despite the arrests, it appeared that over £30million was still missing.

In the winter of 2008, Ken and Valerie Crow were sitting in their living room watching TV when two men in balaclavas appeared beside them. They calmly asked the couple where the money was but Ken pleaded that he had no idea what they were talking about.

Of course, he did know what money the men were talking about, as the Crow's owned and lived on a small farm outside the village of Golden Green near Tonbridge. Their 14 acre land was the nearest open area of land to where the Securitas robbery had taken place, which was a prime location for potentially burying some of the loot.

After tying the couple up and searching the house, the men disappeared as quietly as they had appeared. In February 2009, exactly three years after the robbery, and with the main players already in prison, the Crows were visited again.

On a cold Winter's morning, Ken went for a walk on his land and found holes all over the place. Someone believed the missing £30million had been buried somewhere on the farm and were going to any length to find it.

Ken and his wife were never involved in the robbery, but someone, somewhere, assumed the money was on the farm. The couple still receive threatening letters today, asking them where the money is – a fallout from the largest cash robbery in British history.

The plan and the people

MMA fighter Lee Murray was considered to be the mastermind behind the robbery and with the aid of fellow cage fighter, Paul Allen, began putting together a crew to execute their plan. The plan was so extensive that at least 36 people would be involved in it.

Most assisted with the planning stages but were not involved directly in the removal of money from the depot and were let off after becoming witnesses in the investigation. This included two hairdressers who helped disguise the main gang members with prosthetics and fake beards.

Murray and Allen put together a crew of petty criminals that included car salesman Stuart Royle, garage owner Roger Coutts, roofer Lea Rusha, Kosovan-Albanian nightclub doorman Jetmir Bucpapa, company director Ian Bowrem, and Securitas depot insider Emir Hysenaj.

In the hours before the heist got underway, the gang kidnapped the manager of the depot, Colin Dixon, while posing as police officers. They realised they needed someone to let them into the depot, a location that facilitated the collection and distribution of cash across the UK on behalf of the Bank of England.

They abducted him as he was on his way home from work and took him away in a car to a farm where he was interrogated about the layout of the depot before being taken there. At the same time, other members of the gang went to his home, threatening to kill his family if he didn't assist them in getting into the depot.

They bundled his wife and son into a 7.5-tonne lorry and drove to them to the depot at the same time the rest of the gang arrived with Colin. Armed with assault rifles, a way in, and a plan, the gang entered the depot with the lorry. Dixon let them into the building and the gang forced their way in behind him at gunpoint.

They tied up 14 workers along with Dixon's family and started removing as much cash as they could. The gang filled the lorry with almost £53million in 50, 20, and 10 pound notes. They left behind £154million as it wouldn't fit inside the lorry.

They left the depot at 2am on a strict schedule that Murray was keeping check on with a stopwatch. An hour later, the staff triggered an alarm, and news of the biggest robbery on British soil began doing the rounds.

Swift arm of the law

Despite being the mastermind of the robbery, Murray made the error of having accidentally recorded himself plotting the crime on his mobile phone. The error meant that the investigation team put on the case discovered who was responsible with ease.

Within three days, detectives found the two hairdressers who had disguised the gang, and two days after that, the first three members of the gang had been arrested. Crimestoppers had put up a reward of £2million for information about the heist, which undoubtedly helped the case, and was the largest reward of its kind in the UK at the time.

Armed police officers raided the homes of Bucpapa and Rusha and upon finding the evidence they needed, including footage of depot manager Dixon's home, put out an arrest warrant for them. They were caught the next day after a police chase resulted in the suspect's car tyres being shot out.

Due to the high number of peripheral people involved in the robbery, police received numerous tip-offs and turned suspects into witnesses in an attempt to track down the missing £53million. Various tip-offs directed detectives to three locations where a substantial amount of money was found.

A parked car in a car park in Ashford, a garage in Tunbridge Wells, and a mechanic's yard in Welling, yielded results. A total of £19.5million was found in various suitcases and sports bags taken from the locations. Smaller bags of money were found in the suspects homes and family residencies.

With the evidence found at the scenes, police linked the locations to Coutts and Royle who were arrested shortly after. Allen and Murray fled to Morocco and began buying up property and assets with their share of the loot.

Four months later they were captured in a joint international effort and arrested by Moroccan authorities. Company director Bowrem was arrested on a tip-off as he drove his Mercedes around the M25.

He was caught with £1million in cash in the trunk of the car, of which half was made up of notes from the robbery. It was suspected Bowrem was involved to help launder the money through legitimate companies. By that point, the eight main people involved in the robbery were in custody.

Ordered to pay back £1

The eighth person was Hysenaj, who was proven to be the insider working at the Securitas depot. He had secretly filmed the layout of the depot with a small camera attached to his belt. Until his arrest, police suspected that the manager, Colin Dixon, was the inside man, and had set it up for his family to be kidnapped to allay any suspicion against him.

Many charges were dropped against the people who were peripherally involved in the robbery, including some family members, a man who helped paint the van to hide its identity from police, the hairdressers, and a driver who allegedly drove to Spain with some of the cash built into furniture.

Though the eight main players went to trial, the investigation only accounted for £20million of the stolen money which meant that over £30million was still out in the wilds somewhere, hidden away making someone rich.

By January 2008, an unusual collection of six people were convicted of the robbery. Company director Bowrem was sentenced to three years, nine months and was released early to live out the rest of his life, possibly with some hidden money somewhere.

Doorman Bucpapa got 15 years to life and was released in 2020, 12 years later. He moved to Albania and married in a suspiciously lavish wedding ceremony, which caught the interests of the British and Albanian police forces.

In addition to 12 years served, Bucpapa was ordered to pay back just £1 as the courts believed his share had already been found.

Car salesman Royle got life in prison, the insider Hysenaj got 20 years, roofer Rusha got life, and garage owner Coutts also got life.

The masterminds

Murray and Allen had fled to Morocco in the days following the robbery and had planned to live in

Africa off the proceeds. They purchased property, drugs, jewellery and other assets with the money in an attempt to hide it from authorities.

Bizarrely, they had already paid tens of thousands to plastic surgeons to make their facial features different over the course of many years. They were both arrested four months after the robbery. Allen was extradited back to the UK in October 2009 and was sentenced to 18 years in prison. During a secret hearing he was ordered to pay back just £420 as the courts couldn't work out if the money that had already been recovered was Allen's share or not.

Allen was released six years later for good behaviour but as he was one of the mastermind's of the robbery was subject to the same suspicions as Ken and Valerie Crow, where people believed he knew where more of the money was hidden.

In July 2019, Allen was shot twice at a house rented out by comedian Russell Kane. The gunman fired six bullets through the conservatory window in a pre-meditated hit, in front of Allen's wife and child. The gunman fled the scene in a Mercedes that has never been found but not considered to be the same Mercedes belonging to Bowrem.

Allen barely survived after being shot in the throat and chest. The gunman has never been identified but many suspect it was to cover up the fact that Allen knew where most of the missing loot was hidden or buried.

In 2010, the mastermind, Murray, after a successful request to not be extradited to the UK, was sentenced to ten years in a Moroccan prison. During an appeal, partly instigated by the British authorities, the sentence was raised to 25 years.

£30million simply vanished

We know the players, we know what went down, and we know what happened to the robbers. But the mystery still remains – where is the missing £30million? Some of it would have been used by Allen and Murray in an attempt to purchase assets in Morocco and Africa but it would have totalled nowhere near that amount.

There is the belief from detectives involved in the case that the cash would have been spread throughout various criminal networks in the UK and abroad. They also admitted that although the main robbers had been convicted, there may have been other people involved.

Of the 36 people initially arrested for the crime, only the main robbers were convicted, and the others were given plea deals or various agreements to testify against them. Some detectives believe there were other people involved who were never even considered to be suspects.

One theory suggests that at least three people had eloped with much of the cash and were living off the proceeds somewhere in Cyprus or the West Indies, away from prying eyes, and fully integrated into their new communities.

In 2013, in Canterbury, a builder named Malcolm Constable shot himself in the head in his brother's garden, dying of his wound instantly. His brother had long suspected that he was somehow involved in the robbery but it has never been proven.

Someone knows the truth

The robbery is unusual in that many of the robbers were not involved in organised crime and were for want of a better phrase, ordinary people living ordinary lives. Their professions certainly didn't link them with a life of crime.

That a group of essentially small-time crooks managed to pull off the largest cash robbery in British history, and the second-largest cash robbery in the world, is something of an oddity. Even more so that they managed to make £30million disappear into thin air.

The largest cash robbery in history was committed in 2003 when $1billion (USD) was robbed from the Central Bank of Iraq after the U.S. invaded the country. Although it eclipses the Securitas robbery, it remains astonishing that so much cash was stolen on British soil.

The robbers initially faced a massive hurdle. The amount of money they stole in the denominations they did, worked out to half a tonne in weight and would have filled 75 large suitcases. In money-laundering terms, it would have been extremely difficult to hide.

The UK Financial Intelligence Unit seized more than £800million in criminal assets in the years after the Securitas heist, but not one of the notes or assets traced back to the robbery or the perpetrators. It was as if the £30million had simply disappeared into thin air.

Except it didn't, much of the cash would have been buried, hidden or taken abroad through various methods where it was less likely to be traced, hence the detectives belief that other people were involved and were now living abroad.

But there are those who still believe that some of the haul is still buried on the farm belonging to Ken and Valerie Crow, so much so that the farm now has extensive security to stop people digging up their land.

Perhaps the money said to be buried on the Crows land is a smokescreen, a myth perpetuated by the uncaptured robbers behind the heist, who know what really happened to the money, and are living off the proceeds to this day.

The Blackout Killer

During wartime London, as the German bombs were raining down, a serial killer was at work who brought a new kind of darkness to the cold and lonely streets of the British Capital.

There is nothing worse than a city in fear of bombs falling from the sky, except perhaps a serial killer who took advantage of London's darkest hour to feed an evil desire for cold-blooded murder.

Known as the Blackout Killer or the Wartime Ripper, 27-year-old Gordon Cummins finally snapped and went on a killing spree across London that left six women dead and two severely injured, who barely managed to escape his clutches.

Coming just fifty years after the infamous Jack the Ripper murders, Cummins was seen as a new ripper, carving his way through the streets of London. Most of the murders took place in

February 1942 but he was also suspected of killing two more a few months earlier in October 1941.

The air raids across Britain's major cities led to enforced blackout measures at night, blanketing the cities in darkness. It was under this cover of night that the Blackout Killer roamed the wartime streets seeking his innocent victims.

Extravagant persona

The blackouts had been imposed on various cities including London from September 1939 and were put in place to prevent enemy aircraft from being able to identify targets by sight. The blackouts remained in place until some restrictions were lifted in September 1944 as the German war machine weakened.

What set Cummins apart from the rest of his dark peers, was the brutality with which he carried out many of his murders. Some of the victims were so badly mutilated that police first thought they had been victims of a German bomb.

Born at the tail-end of the First World War, North Yorkshire-raised Cummins spent his childhood under the watchful eye of hard-working parents. His father ran a school for mentally challenged teenagers, and his mother was a housewife to four children.

Cummins had an unremarkable childhood but sought a career in chemistry before moving to

Newcastle when he was 18 to take a job as an industrial chemist. Due to his poor time-keeping and anti-social behaviour, most-likely developed from his family's closeness to the delinquent school, he failed to keep down a job for more than a few months.

When he was 20, Cummins moved to London and took various jobs but found himself drawn into the large social life the city offered. His love for clubs, bars, and London women, led to him developing a persona for himself that lifted him from his working class roots to something he believed was more desirable.

He worked on a posh London accent and told wild stories of nights with multiple women and a fake heritage designed to show others how better he was than them. His extravagant persona was funded by petty theft, lifting him from his beer-swigging peers into a champagne lifestyle.

The Duke

At 21, Cummins joined the Royal Air Force and his posh persona led to many nicknames including The Duke and The Count. Though he annoyed most of his comrades with tales of grandeur, he trained hard enough to be selected for flight duty by the RAF selection board.

He also married Marjorie Stevens in 1936 but they never had children and their marriage was more out of convenience than love. She would continue to believe her husband was innocent of any crimes right up until her own death many years later.

Shortly before his arrest, Cummins was due to report for duty at an Air Crew Receiving Centre in Regent's Park, where he would have ultimately sat behind the controls of a Spitfire. But the Duke had gone down a path of murder and brutality that to this day raises the hairs on the back of the neck.

During the time of the first London murders in October 1941, Cummins was stationed in Colerne, Wiltshire, but whenever he went on leave, would head straight for central London to use prostitutes and revel in his own tales of magnificence and showmanship.

On the morning of 14th October 1941, following a bombing raid, workmen were searching through the rubble of a bombed house in Hampstead Road, close to Regents Park, when they stumbled upon a body. It was not unusual to find bodies in London during the war but there was something different about this one.

On top of some debris was the nude body of 19-year-old secretary Maple Churchward but she didn't show any signs of having been hurt during the bombing. Unsure of what they were looking at, the workmen called in the police, who confirmed that Maple had been strangled to death with her own knickers.

Despite being found nude, she had not been sexually assaulted. Police learned that Maple commonly slept with British servicemen, sometimes for money, other times for fun. She had last been seen at a bar in nearby Camden the previous evening.

Four days later, on the 17th, 48-year-old Edith Humphries was found by a friend lying in bed suffering from severe wounds. She had been stabbed in the head, hit with a heavy object multiple times, and her throat had been cut.

Edith was alive when she was rushed to hospital but died shortly after. There was no forced entry to her home and due to the closeness of both women's murders, police suspected the same killer had been responsible. Edith too was seen at a Central London bar the night before her murder.

The mutilator

Due to the severity of the war over London, the two murders were put on the backburner. During the following three months, Cummins was stationed at RAF St. John's Wood, commonly known as RAF Regents Park – a perfect location for him to escalate the murders.

On 8th February 1942, after a brief visit to his wife in nearby Southwark, Cummins headed out into war-torn London. A day later, another victim was found dead in an air-raid shelter. 41-year-old pharmacist Evelyn Hamilton was last seen drinking wine celebrating her 41st birthday at Marble Arch.

As she walked back to her boarding house, Cummins befriended and lured her to the air-raid shelter, where he became violent. He ripped off her clothes and manually strangled her to death. The autopsy showed that she tried to fight him off but was not sexually assaulted.

Her body was found by an electrician the following morning. Police discovered her handbag had been stolen, which may have contained upwards of £80, worth over £4,000 today. They learned that she was leaving London for Lincolnshire the next day and was winding up her personal affairs.

That same evening on 9th February, 34-year-old married nightclub hostess and prostitute Evelyn Oatley was approached by Cummins as she waited outside a restaurant in Shaftesbury. Just before midnight, the pair were seen entering an apartment building at 153 Wardour Street by another tenant.

The same tenant heard Oatley's radio turned up loud after midnight as Cummins was killing her and mutilating her body. He beat and strangled her into unconsciousness before cutting her throat from ear to ear. He then stripped her and laid her flat on the bed with her head hanging over the edge.

Then, with a razor blade, tin opener, and piece of a broken mirror, Cummins cut up her body, before raping her with an electric torch and curling tongs. Evidence found at the scene suggested he had used a total of seven blades to slice her body, which was found the next morning by electric meter workers.

The whistler

Already tainted by the horrors of war, police found fingerprints on the tin opener, mirror, and other items belonging to Oatley. But when they checked the fingerprints on the police database, there was no match, and for good reason – Cummins had never been arrested or convicted of a crime.

Which makes his sudden killing of many women that much stranger. On the next day, the 11th, 43-year-old prostitute Margaret Florence Lowe was murdered at her flat in Gosfield Street, Marylebone. She had last been seen by a neighbour in the early hours of the morning, accompanied by a client.

The same neighbour heard the client leave about an hour later, whistling away to himself, as if he'd had a night of fun. Lowe's body wouldn't be found until two days later when her 15-year-old daughter arrived home to find her on a bloody bed.

Her nude body had been positioned in such a way that she was on her back with her legs apart and knees bent upward. She had been brutally beaten to death and strangled with a silk stocking. And if police thought Oatley's murder was horrific, it was nothing compared to Lowe's.

Cummins had mutilated Lowe, partly when she was alive, but mostly after she had died. He used a razor blade, kitchen knife, dinner knife, and a fire poker, to stab and slice her body. All four weapons were left embedded in her body or nearby on the bed.

Her stomach had been sliced open with such severity that her organs were exposed, along with multiple lacerations and cuts to her groin. A large wax candle had also been inserted into her. That the suspect walked away from the scene whistling happily sent chills down the investigators spines.

Unstoppable

Fingerprints were lifted and matched those from the Oatley crime scene. Autopsies confirmed the suspect was left-handed, which Cummins was, but he was able to hide himself away in the arms of RAF Regent's Park.

One day after Lowe's horrific death, on 12th February, 25-year-old prostitute Catherine Mulcahy was attacked by Cummins in her own home, after he had paid for her services. As Mulcahy stripped, Cummins attacked her and pushed her to the bed attempting to strangle her.

But Mulcahy was strong enough to fight him off and ran screaming from the flat. She later claimed that Cummins's eyes had changed from a well-to-do gentleman to a monster within seconds. Cummins exited the flat and tried to give her more money then fled before police arrived.

It was perhaps a fortunate case of luck that Cummins had forgotten to put back on his RAF belt, which was found in Mulcahy's apartment. The same evening, Cummins hooked up with 32-year-old prostitute Doris Jouannet, who took him back to her flat in Bayswater. She had referred to Cummins as a client she called '*The Captain*'.

The following day, Jouannet's husband with the help of a friend who was a police officer, broke down her bedroom door and discovered her nude body on the bed she used to entertain clients. The same brutality had been inflicted on Jouannet,

She had been strangled with a silk stocking, her jaw had been broken off due to the savagery of the attack, and her body had been mutilated with various sharp instruments, including a razor blade and multiple knives. Some of the flesh underneath her breasts had been carved off.

Once again, fingerprints taken from the scene matched those of the other murders. But police were already closing in due to Cummins having left the RAF belt at Mulcahy's flat.

Prelude to an end

The press initially gave little service to the story of the murderer, but with the killings so close together, Cummins was referred to as the Blackout Killer, and the following day made headlines across the entire country.

Even with police investigating him, and the press writing about the murders, for some reason known only to Cummins, he just couldn't stop killing, and less than a day after Jouannet's murder, he attacked another woman.

On the 13th, Cummins lured Margaret Heywood to join him for a drink in a bar in Piccadilly. When they left the bar, he attempted to forcibly direct Heywood to a nearby air raid shelter but she tried to fight him off. Cummins then pushed her into a doorway and strangled her into unconsciousness.

The attack was stopped when a passing beer bottle deliveryman spotted Cummins rifling through Heywood's handbag. The deliveryman came to the rescue forcing Cummins to flee, and in doing so he left behind his RAF gas mask and rucksack in the doorway. To cover himself later, Cummins stole another serviceman's gas mask and rucksack.

Fortunately, Heywood survived the attack and would later be able to identify Cummins. When police got hold of the gas mask and rucksack, they contacted the local RAF bases who ultimately led them to Cummins, due to the issue numbers on the military gear.

On Valentine's morning, Cummins was arrested but concocted a fake story that he was out drinking whisky with another serviceman whose name he coincidentally couldn't recall. He claimed to have no memory of attacking Heywood but wished to apologise to her if he had done.

While he was under arrest for committing grievous bodily harm, detectives realised they could have the Blackout Killer in custody, so they jumped into full-on investigatory mode to prove it.

Irrefutable evidence

The RAF Regent's Park passbook was signed by Cummins on all the nights that the murders and attacks happened, but fellow servicemen claimed they all had each other's backs and falsified documents with pencil should any one of them return after a military-enforced curfew.

Police later discovered that Cummins and other servicemen would sneak out of the base at night and not return until the early hours. When police searched his belongings they found most of the proof they were looking for.

Cummings had been taking souvenirs from each of his victims including a metal cigarette case belonging to Oatley along with a picture of her mother. There were traces of blood on one of his unwashed shirts, and his military uniform had traces of brick dust only found in the air raid shelter were Hamilton's body was found.

But more importantly, all the fingerprints belonging to the suspect in the four February murders were a match with Cummins. They also discovered that new £1 notes had been given to Mulcahy by her attacker. Investigators tracked the serial numbers and discovered the notes were brand new and had been issued via the RAF base to Cummins.

Heywood identified Cummins in a line-up and the police had everything they needed to lay multiple counts of murder at his feet. In front of them was not only one of the most brutal killers of 1940s London but a terrifying serial killer who offered no real motive for his crimes beyond circumstance.

Serial killer

Cummins still maintained his innocence when he was charged with murder on the 16th of February and put together various stories to lay the blame at the feet of other servicemen who had *'clearly'* swapped RAF-issued clothing and accessories with him to pin the blame on him.

In April 1942, Cummins went on trial for the murder of Oatley and pleaded not guilty. With all the witnesses, autopsies, and forensic evidence, there was no way Cummins was going to get away with it.

He was found guilty of the murder of Oatley, and in the interests of the British public, was sentenced to death. On 25th June 1942, Cummins was led to the gallows at Wandsworth prison where he was hanged. He maintained his innocence right up until the end.

He was eventually linked with the other murders, the two in October 1941 and three in February 1942. That he was already sentenced to death meant that any other convictions would not have changed the ultimate outcome.

Cummins was the only convicted murderer to be executed during an air raid. He remains one of Britain's most curious and brutal serial killer's, having claimed one more victim than Jack the Ripper, bringing darkness to a city where there were already horrors at every turn.

Burning of Mary Channing

A young woman obsessed with free money, parties, and multiple lovers, poisoned her husband and was burned at the stake for her troubles in front of thousands of people.

Born in 1687 to hard working and wealthy parents in Dorchester, Mary Brookes (later Channing) was provided with a healthy and happy childhood. Though Dorchester would evolve to become the jewel in the crown of Dorset, it was already marred by darkness.

Just two years before Mary's birth, 312 prisoners of the Monmouth Rebellion were tried in the town, leading to 74 men being hung in public. It was an age of war and violence under the ever-persisting threat of witchcraft.

Despite her somewhat wealthy childhood, Mary had a most unremarkable upbringing, with one of the highlights being that she was taught to read and write, a rarity in Dorchester for a young girl at the time.

But when she reached her teenage years, Mary was already unkempt, untidy in appearance and known to be sexually active. Her parents constantly opened new businesses to keep the family going and avoid the pitfalls of 17th Century working class Britons, leaving Mary mostly on her own.

Husband to control her

It was this lack of parental direction that many blamed for Mary's later actions, enabled by parents who believed in materialism over spiritualism. With their new wealth, they sent her on visits to London to broaden her view of the world and experience what could be possible for her future.

After many trips around the country, she settled back in Dorchester and spent her time in the company of women and men who were free and spirited like her, much to her parent's distaste. She fell for one of her young neighbours and gave him lavish gifts to win his affection.

Their sexual encounters were so passionate that the man's own neighbours complained of the noise they would make. When Mary's parents received word of her unruly behaviour, they made the decision to marry her off – but not to the neighbour.

Her parents chose a grocer named Thomas Channing, as they knew the family. They believed that a husband like Thomas would be able to control her and give her a better standing in the town beyond the mischief and anti-social behaviour she was beginning to elicit.

On 15th January 1704, 17-year-old Mary reluctantly married Thomas at a downbeat wedding ceremony. Thomas had tried to change her ways but failed from the outset. Within a month of being married, Mary was carrying on her love affair with the young neighbour.

Lewd and indecent

As her hatred of her parents grew, and needing money to continue her illicit affair, she tried to convince some of her friends to help rob her own parents. They didn't agree and word spread further around town that Mary was leading a life of crime and was bringing the name of Dorchester into disrepute.

To facilitate her affair, she paid off local homeowners so she could use their homes for meetings with her lover. As her passion for adulterous relationships grew, she found comfort in the arms of many different men and gained access to their homes, lives, and friends.

Soon, Mary was known around town as the source of parties and reckless abandon. As such, homeowners were more willing to rent out their homes in order to lay on lavish parties that involved dancing, alcohol, and sex.

By this point, the Channing family had become aware of Mary's lifestyle and privately turned against her but stood by Thomas in the hope that he might receive financial favour from Mary's family. Mary's father then said he would bestow nothing on them but his blessing.

As a humbled wife, Mary had to travel around the country accompanying Thomas in his business meetings and work. But whenever she got the opportunity, she returned back to Dorchester and into the arms of her many lovers, returning to her pre-marriage ways.

It was written in a story about Mary after her execution that at many private engagements, her conversation was so lewd and her actions so indecent that even the men who were present were embarrassed and ashamed to be in her company.

The poisoning

When Thomas's father cut off a line of credit to Thomas and Mary, it set in motion a plan of murder. Unable to afford her lavish lifestyle without the financial assistance from her husband and his family, Mary decided to kill her husband and claim his inheritance and wealth for herself.

On Monday 16th April 1705, Mary purchased some mercury from an apothecary's assistant, when she was told there was no rat poison available. The next morning, as Thomas sat down for breakfast, Mary served him a dish of rice milk laced with a substantial part of the mercury, a toxic metal that is poisonous when consumed in large quantities.

Just a couple of spoonful's was all it took to make Thomas ill, due to the amount of poison that Mary had put into the milk. She washed everything up and wiped down any trace of evidence as Thomas became violently ill, vomiting in the front garden of their home.

Bizarrely, a neighbour's dog thought the vomit was food and ate some of it. When the dog became ill as well, the neighbours suspected foul play was afoot. Though terribly ill, Thomas remained alive but bedridden. As the days passed, and Mary fed him more of the poison, Thomas concluded that his own wife was indeed poisoning him. He wrote a will leaving his entire estate to his father, and just one shilling to Mary, a token amount to acknowledge that she was not to receive a shilling more.

By the Saturday, Thomas had succumbed to the pain of the poison and passed away having suffered terribly. His father was already suspicious and ordered an autopsy to ascertain the true cause of death. When it turned out that Thomas had poison coursing through his veins, there was only one suspect.

Search party

The local police searched Dorchester for Mary but initially couldn't find her. Realising she had been rumbled, Mary eloped four miles to the next parish where she spent most of the day in a wooded area hiding among the trees.

Thomas's father raised a search party to rampage through Dorchester and the surrounding areas to find the witch that had killed his son. They searched the woods where she had been seen but Mary had secretly, and under cover of night, returned to Dorchester.

When she was captured, she claimed she never realised her husband had died and was innocent of any accusations laid at her feet. She was charged with Thomas's murder and held in the local jail as investigators tried to work out the truth of what had happened.

One of Mary's brothers lied to police and said that Thomas had asked him to get the poison so he could use it for his business. The story was almost believed except at that exact time, the apothecary assistant had come forward and stated that Mary had purchased mercury.

Orrible British True Crime Volume 2

The trial began on 28th July 1705 in Dorchester where Mary pleaded not guilty to the murder of her husband. Many witnesses were called forward to testify against Mary's character and her unwanted relationship with her husband. The fact that Thomas had changed the will shortly before his death meant he became a posthumous witness in his own murder.

Mary was seen preparing all of Thomas's meals before his death. She was also seen hiding from the search party that went out to look for her. It was expected she would be found guilty but the sentence was somewhat unexpected.

Maumbury Rings

Her lover also gave evidence that he was with her on many nights while she was married and that she spoke of her husband with disdain. She had also gifted her lover and others in the town expensive goods, paid for by her husband's finances, yet she would not bestow her husband with such gifts.

The nail in the coffin was the testimony of the apothecary assistant who confirmed that Mary was looking for rat poison but purchased mercury – the poison found in Thomas's blood. Unusually for the time period, Mary acted as her own defence and questioned the witnesses herself, which didn't help as she was found guilty.

She was sentenced to death, to be burned alive at the stake. However, unknown to the court, Mary was pregnant with the child of an unidentified father. Her sentence was postponed until after she gave birth. When her son arrived, her family begged the courts for leniency and asked for a pardon which was never given despite an appeal.

During the appeal, she managed to get herself baptised by a local clergyman, who also begged the courts to change the sentence. The clergyman wrote to the Bishop of Bristol but no further intervention was to come.

On 21st March 1706, Mary Channing was led to the neolithic henge site of Maumbury Rings in the town to be executed. Two men had already been executed in the hour before her, one for stealing and another for murder.

A crowd of thousands had gathered for Mary's execution, with some reports stating as many as 10,000, though exact numbers have never been agreed. When pressed for a confession, she continued to maintain her innocence.

At five in the afternoon, Mary was fixed to the stake and manually strangled to death – a small mercy requested by the church. When she was found to be dead, the firewood was kindled and the crowds watched her burn to ash.

Peter Tobin & Bible John

Three murders in the late 1960s linked to the mysterious Bible John remain unsolved to this day, with a strong suspicion that serial killer Peter Tobin was the man behind the unidentified murderer.

For many years, there was a seemingly obvious connection between a serial killer and various unsolved murders, but decades later, it seems the connections have been cut and there could have been two serial killers in Scotland in the late 1960s, one of whom has never been caught.

Scottish serial killer and rapist Peter Britton Tobin killed three women over an extended period of time and raped many others. On 10th February 1991, 15-year-old schoolgirl Vicky Hamilton vanished from a bus stop in Falkirk, Scotland, and was stabbed to death by Tobin.

Realising heat was on him, he fled Scotland to a new flat at 50 Irvine Drive, Margate, Kent, and in a macabre display of ownership, took Hamilton's body with him. He later buried her corpse in the back garden of the property.

Six months later, in Essex, England, 18-year-old student Dinah McNicol vanished while hitchhiking with her boyfriend, who was dropped off at a different location while McNicol stayed in the car. Tobin was later confirmed to have been the driver and her eventual killer.

In the months that followed, regular withdrawals were made from her bank account to the maximum amount of £250 each time. Tobin had forced McNicol to hand over her PIN before killing her, though his motive for murder was primarily sexual and not robbery.

She too was buried in the back garden near to the decomposed corpse of Hamilton. It would be another 16 years before their remains were uncovered following Tobin's subsequent arrest for their murders.

The Jesus Fellowship

In 1993, two years after escaping justice for the murders, he raped two 14-year-old-girls at his new flat in Leigh Park, Havant, a large residential area just north of Portsmouth. The two girls went to visit a neighbour who wasn't in so asked to wait in Tobin's flat.

He then held them at knifepoint, forced alcohol down their throats and raped them. He stabbed one of them and turned the gas on in the house to kill them. The two girls survived the attack and went straight to the police.

Tobin went on the run immediately as the girls had identified him and were obviously found to have been raped in Tobin's home. To avoid police he joined a religious sect in Coventry, named the Jesus Fellowship.

Also known as the Jesus Army, the group – or cult, as some called them – were part of the British New Church movement and were founded in 1969 to spread the Christian message to people directly by using street-based evangelism.

By 2007, there were said to be an estimated 3,500 followers in 24 separate congregations. By 2019, the group came under fire for its leaders having committed sexual assaults against children and young women during the 1970s.

Fitting then, that Tobin was part of the group, living on one of their communal properties, hidden from the long arm of the law. Today, there are still around 200 followers who live in communal buildings owned by the group.

While on a trip to Brighton, when his car was spotted parked up on the seafront, Tobin was arrested for the attacks on the two girls. In 1994, he was sentenced to 14 years in prison but only served 10 and had escaped justice for the murders of Hamilton and McNicol, as he was never connected to them at the time.

Body in the church

He was released in 2004 and sent back to Scotland, where he disappeared from the authorities by exploiting open-door policies at various churches and religious groups. He went by many different names in order to remain off-the-grid and hid the fact he was on the sex offenders' register.

He became an expert at hiding himself among fringe religious groups, but there was a darkness inside of Tobin that saw him needing to commit more crimes, and it would come at the expense of the groups that veiled him from the world.

In September 2006, less than two years after his release, he attacked and killed 23-year-old Polish student Angelika Kluk, who was staying in the accommodation building of a church that Tobin was working at.

She was raped, beaten and stabbed to death in a frenzied attack that the coroner claimed was one of the worst he had ever seen. Tobin hid her body in an underground chamber in the floor of the church, near to the confessional booth, but his haphazard attempt at dumping the body led to his downfall.

A few days later, Kluk's body was discovered, after a churchgoer noticed the flooring had been disturbed. The coroner later confirmed that Kluk may have been alive when she was buried in the chamber.

Knowing police were closing in on him, and in an attempt to trick authorities, Tobin admitted himself to hospital under a false name, and with a fictitious complaint. But police were already aware of what Tobin looked like, and word was put out to various authorities around England. He was arrested shortly after Kluk's body was found.

Tobin was charged and went to trial in the Spring of 2007, where he was found guilty of the rape and murder of Kluk and was sentenced to a minimum of 21 years in prison. He believed he had escaped justice for the murders of Hamilton and McNicol – until investigators looked closer.

Operation Anagram

Realising Tobin had already been convicted of rape and attempted murder, the investigation looked at older cases that he might have been involved in. Due to the number of properties that Tobin was known to have lived in, forensic searches of numerous houses and flats were undertaken across the country, including one at the seaside town of Southsea, Hampshire.

On 14th November 2007, police confirmed that human remains had been unearthed at Tobin's former residence at 50 Irvine Drive. The first remains to be discovered were that of 15-year-old Hamilton. At the same time, Essex Police opened a cold case for Dinah McNicol and linked up with the Tobin investigation.

A few days after Hamilton's remains were discovered, McNicol's remains were discovered in the grounds of the same property. The then owners of the house had no idea they were living with the corpses of two teenage girls.

In November 2008, Tobin was transferred to a court in Dundee, Scotland, where he was convicted for the murder of Hamilton. After a trial which lasted a month, Tobin had his 21-year sentence increased to a 30 years minimum.

'Yet again you have shown yourself to be unfit to live in a decent society. It is hard for me to convey the loathing and revulsion that ordinary people will feel for what you have done.' – The judge in Hamilton's murder trial.

For McNicol's murder, Tobin went to trial in 2009, in an Essex court. Unusually, Tobin's defence offered no evidence in his favour. It took less than 15 minutes for the jury to find him guilty, and he was sentenced to an additional life term.

On the same day that Tobin was convicted of his third murder, police reopened multiple cold cases under the banner of Operation Anagram. Investigators came to believe that Tobin may have been involved in at least 13 more murders.

It was then he was linked to the Bible John Murders in Glasgow, which remain unsolved to this day. The three murders from 1968 to 1969 were similar in style to Tobin's method of killing, and he would have been in and around the area at the time.

The artist photofit of Bible John matched photos of how Tobin looked at the time. Eyewitnesses claimed that the suspect had one tooth missing on the right-hand side of his mouth. Tobin had one tooth removed in the late 1960s, in the same place that matched eyewitness accounts.

He got the name of Bible John because it was suspected that he went to rape his victims but found them in the middle of their menstrual cycle, so he killed them instead. Tobin also left Glasgow just a few weeks after the final known Bible John murder. But was Tobin the victim of Henry Lee Lucas syndrome or really the beast behind Bible John?

Henry Lee Lucas syndrome

Henry Lee Lucas was an American serial killer who claimed at least three lives from 1960 to 1983, though he is positively linked to eight in total. When Lucas confessed to 600 murders, police forces all over the United States began looking at their cold case files.

With Lucas confessing to hundreds of murders, the police realised they could clear up their outstanding cold cases and pin them on Lucas. And so, at one point, over 3,000 murders were linked to Lucas, which of course was absurd.

However, at least 213 of those cases were eventually cleared and marked as solved. For a short while, whenever a cold case investigation was reopened, many police forces attempted to clear their unsolved cases by linking to them Lucas.

The same thing happens to two British serial killers on a regular basis, child killer Robert Black, and of course, Peter Tobin. Though there is rarely much evidence beyond circumstantial to connect them to the cold case murders, they are connected nonetheless and ultimately linked to them.

Bible John's victims were picked up from the Barrowland Ballroom in Glasgow, that remains open today as The Barrowlands. Despite one of the longest manhunts in Scottish history, the murders remain unsolved and the suspect unidentified.

The Bible John murders made Scottish crime history when a composite of the suspect was released publicly for the first time. Unfortunately, police recently confirmed that DNA evidence from the three Bible John murders had deteriorated due to incorrect storage of the samples.

This means that if Tobin was Bible John, then without a confession, it would be difficult to now prove. Operation Anagram hit full speed in 2010, as police forces across the United Kingdom checked DNA against cold cases and followed up on missing people that might have been connected with Tobin.

Likely had killed many more

In the end, multiple murder cases of teenage girls and women were reopened. During interviews with Tobin, psychiatrists and profilers suggested he most likely had killed many more, beyond the three he had been convicted for.

On Wednesday 15th May 1980, 22-year-old Eastbourne College student Jessie Earl had disappeared from her bedsit and failed to return home the next morning. The London born student was known to take long walks up to Beachy Head where she would read and write about nature.

So when she disappeared, and a police search turned up no trace of her, it was suggested she had become part of the saddening suicide statistics that had haunted Beachy Head for centuries. Until her remains were discovered on the cliff top nine years later.

Her death was included as one of the cold cases in Operation Anagram. Though similarities were found between Earl's case and Tobin's confirmed victims, there was not enough solid evidence to convict him of the murder, which to this day remains unsolved.

The operation diminished in 2011 when they failed to positively link any more victims to Tobin. While in prison, Tobin boasted to a psychiatrist that he had ended the lives of 48 people.

But if Tobin was not Bible John, as the evidence suggests, then who was? At the time of the murders, a man calling himself John White was suspected to be the killer but because his teeth didn't match that of the eye-witness accounts, he was discounted.

John White was a fake name, he had been seen arguing with women, made regular visits to the Barrowland Ballroom, and fitted the profile of the killer. However, in 2005, 'White' came forward to offer a DNA sample which then removed him from the suspect pool.

Unidentified serial killer

In 1983, police received an anonymous phone call from a Dutch man who claimed his friend was Bible John. He believed it because of his friend's demeanour, activity in Glasgow around the time of the killings, and his love of the Barrowland Ballroom. No suspects were ever identified following the call.

In 1969, at the time of the murders, Hannah Martin was raped by a man she met at the Ballroom. She would go on to give birth to the child of the rapist, who she believed was Peter

Tobin. Though no DNA of the child was ever provided, if the story were true, then the child's DNA could prove who Bible John really was – or wasn't.

The World's End Murderer, Angus Sinclair, was also connected to the Bible John murders. Sinclair, who was linked to eight murders up until 1978, was already active in 1961 in Glasgow when he killed his eight-year-old neighbour. He was convicted of her murder but was out of prison six years later, at around the time of the Bible John murders.

Yet again, there was no solid evidence to connect Sinclair to Bible John. Many more suspects have been linked to the mysterious killer but Peter Tobin remains the prime candidate. Though his health is deteriorating, as he remains alive in 2022, there is still hope that a death-bed confession could be forthcoming.

If not, and Bible John was not Tobin, then an unidentified serial killer got away with murder for over half a century. Despite the huge ongoing interest in both Tobin and Bible John, the murders of three women in Glasgow from 1968 to 1969, remain unsolved to this day, and a footnote in a wider story of multiple serial killers.

Notting Hill Murder of Vera Page

A ten-year-old girl was abducted and murdered in Notting Hill, leading to a 100-year-old cold case, which despite a strong suspect and solid investigatory work, remains officially unsolved to this day.

Vera was a 10-year-old girl who lived in Notting Hill with her family. On the day of her murder, 14th December 1931, she was visiting nearby relatives when she left to walk the 50-metre distance home. It was the last time she was seen alive.

After a large search of the area, a milkman discovered her body in the undergrowth two days later, a mile away from her home. She had been raped and manually strangled to death. Despite a large and ongoing investigation into her murder, no suspect has ever been caught and her murder remains unsolved.

Born to a working class family in Hammersmith, London, on 13th April 1921, she was raised as an only child by parents who doted on her. Her father, Charles Page, was a railway worker, and her mother, Isabel, stayed at home as a housewife, a product of 1920s England, they moved to a small property in Notting Hill shortly after Vera's birth.

To supplement the family income, Isabel would take in lodgers but they were usually people known to the family, rather than all-out strangers. In January 1931, they moved to a larger three-storey house in Notting Hill, where they resided in rooms across the lower two floors, with other residents above them.

Arthur and Annie Rush were one of the couple's that lived above them and had been there for over two decades when the Page's moved in. One of their sons, 41-year-old Percival Orlando Rush, would frequent the property on many occasions and would eventually become the prime suspect in Vera's disappearance.

Murder & the milkman

On that fateful afternoon in 1931, aged 10, Vera disappeared on the walk back home after visiting her auntie. When she failed to return home, the alarm was raised. It had only been 45 minutes from the time she had left her aunties home to the time she was known to be missing.

Less than an hour was all it took for her abductor to remove her from her family and the life she knew. By 10.30pm, Charles reported his daughter missing to police. He helped put together a search team of relatives and locals to look for her and they worked through the night to no avail.

By the following morning on the 15th, the press had got wind of the story and soon enough the disappearance of Vera Page had gone national. Despite being seen by a school-friend near a chemist, no-one else had seen her in the short distance from her auntie's house to her family home.

In the dark early hours of the morning on the 16th, Joseph Smith, a milkman returning from his duties, stumbled across something he never expected to see. In the front garden of a home near to Holland Park, he saw the body of a child in the undergrowth, covered by her own coat.

There had been no attempt to hide the body and it was on full display for everyone to see. Realising what he was looking at and stunned by the marble-like complexion of the child's face, Joseph raised the alarm.

When police identified the body as Vera's, the abduction became a murder investigation. Distraught at their loss, Vera's parents did all they could to help find the killer, by speaking about it in the press and helping investigators at every turn.

Unfortunately, it meant that Charles became a suspect in his daughter's death but police needed proof. Wedged against Vera's inner elbow were the remnants of a finger bandage with traces of ammonia, which would later prove vital in seeking a suspect. It appeared the killer had a bandage on his finger that had come off when he placed the body in the garden.

A local killer

An autopsy was carried out which unearthed new details. Due to the variation in weather in the two days from being abducted to being found, it was concluded that Vera's body had been kept with her captor for the two days she was missing.

Using the weather patterns and corresponding it with the amount of weathering on Vera's body, it suggested she had been dumped in the undergrowth just two hours before she was discovered.

The autopsy found traces of coal dust and candle wax on her coat and body, which led investigators to believe she had been kept in a coal shed or cellar until being removed and placed in the garden. This combined with the bandage added to an ever-growing stack of evidence, except they had no suspect.

It was confirmed that Vera had been raped and manually strangled to death in the hours following her disappearance, which meant she had lain dead for at least 40 hours.

Detectives believed the man was local to the area, as he would not have been able to keep Vera's body for two days and place her in the garden if he didn't know the area. The placement of the body, away from prying eyes but in a very public location meant that the killer had good local geographical knowledge.

The owner of the house and the milkman confirmed the timeline of when the body must have been placed. The owner, who was an early-riser, collected the milk from the milkman at 5.30am. Neither the milkman nor the owner saw the body then.

When the milkman was returning along the same road at 7.50am, he noticed the body. The owner said she would have seen it before 5.30am if it had been there. This meant the killer had a two hour window to secretly place the body in the garden.

Large investigation

Due to the public outrage at the murder, the pressure on police to find the killer was mounting but the outpouring of grief led to thousands of people attending Vera's funeral. The investigation went house to house around Notting Hill, Kensington, and Holland Park, to speak to as many people as they could.

Over the coming weeks, police took approximately 3,000 witness statements and interviewed over 1,000 people in relation to the murder. Nothing solid came up until one of the later witness statements gave hope that the killer was about to be caught.

At 6.30am on the morning of the 16th, a homeowner was looking out her window when she saw a local man pushing a full wheelbarrow, with its contents covered by a red tablecloth. The homeowner didn't think anything of it until the police spoke to her.

The local man she saw was Percival *'Percy'* Orlando Rush – whose parents lived on the floor above the Page's home. Another witness said that the door to a large coal shed near to where the body was discovered was left open on the morning of the discovery.

The coal shed had no electrical lighting which meant only candles could be used to illuminate the shed, one of the ways that caused traces of candle wax to be found on Vera's body. With the name of a possible suspect, the location the body was stored in, and solid witness statements, police went all in on Percy Rush.

Percival Rush

Rush was a married 41-year-old launderette worker who came into contact with ammonia on a daily basis. He used to live in the same property as the Page's and would regularly return to visit his parents on the top floor, which meant he had a key to the property.

Rush admitted that he talked to Vera many times but had not seen her in the weeks leading up to her murder. More importantly for the investigation, Rush had damaged his little finger a few days before Vera was killed, and had worn a finger bandage, similar to the one that had been found wedged underneath Vera's elbow.

Two days after the body was found, Rush was arrested and questioned at Notting Hill police station where he proclaimed his innocence but agreed with what the police had found out. He didn't deny hurting his finger or knowing Vera but denied he was the killer.

With circumstantial evidence laid at his feet, Rush was charged with the murder and sent to trial but it didn't go to plan for the prosecution, as there simply was not enough evidence to convict him. Rush had hurt his finger at work on the 9th of December and his colleagues said he took it off a couple of days later and was not wearing one on the 14th, the day of Vera's disappearance.

The bandage found on Vera was a perfect fit for Rush's finger but according to a forensic analyst the material used was slightly different to the samples taken from Rush's home during a search by police.

Due to a procedural error, when going house to house, police had told Rush about the bandage, before he was a suspect, which would have given Rush ample time to get rid of any evidence. If Rush was the killer, then the release of confidential information by the police may have resulted in Rush getting away with it.

Unidentified murderer

Despite the witness seeing him pushing a wheelbarrow, there were no other witness statements putting him in the road where the garden was at the time the body was dumped. Local chemists reported they didn't sell Rush or his family the type of bandage found at the scene.

The owner of the coal shed was Thomas O'Conner who had ended his tenancy on it five days before the murder. He had taken the shed's padlocks with him which meant the coal shed would have been unlocked before the body was placed there.

There was simply not enough evidence to prove Rush had killed Vera. The jury agreed that the evidence was circumstantial at best, leading to Rush's acquittal.

For decades after, Rush was vilified as the killer of Vera, despite being acquitted of murder. He died in Ealing in 1961, having claimed his innocence at every opportunity. He had left the courts as a free man but no other suspect was found, and if Rush had killed her then he got away with murder.

If he didn't, then an unidentified killer was let free to walk the streets of Central London, and with the type of murder it was, it wouldn't have been a surprise if the killer had struck again, somewhere and at some time in history. Vera Page's abduction and murder remains officially unsolved.

The Bikini Bloodbath Murder

On the hottest day of the century, a woman sunbathing in her bikini had her throat cut by an unidentified attacker, then left in a pool of blood for her husband to find.

The UK's not really known for consistency in its weather patterns and seasons, but 1990 was a little different. On 3rd August of that year, temperatures reached a scorching 37.1C (98.8F), making it one of the hottest days of the 20th Century.

The usual things happened; people got sunburnt, suffered heatstroke, or drank too much alcohol and passed out in the sun, to wake up stuck to the stones on the beaches around the country. But in Darlington, County Durham, murder clouded the skies.

44-year-old mother of three, Ann Heron, like many others on that fateful Friday, was taking advantage of the weather and sunbathing in her garden. Unlike many others, Ann was brutally murdered by an unidentified killer.

Born Ann Cockburn in 1946 in Glasgow, she moved to England in 1984 when she met the love of her life, Peter Heron, who also had three children. They got married in a lavish ceremony and moved into Aeolian House, a large country property in Middleton St George, near to Darlington.

Ann was a part-time care assistant at a nursing home, while Peter worked as the CEO of GE Stiller Transport, a haulage firm on the outskirts of the town. They lived a happy life, with a growing family, solid social standing, and were well-liked in the community.

There was nothing in their lives that suggested a motive for what happened next but someone, whether by opportunity or planning, decided to end her life in the most brutal of ways.

Timeline of murder

Peter left the home and went to his workplace at the haulage firm, he arrived as always before 9am, such was his dedication to good time-keeping. An hour later, Ann, who had the day off, met up with a friend, Sheila Eagle, and went into Darlington centre to shop for items for a party later that day.

Just before 1pm, and as he always did, Peter went home and had lunch with Ann, no doubt discussing how hot the day was becoming. There's nothing the British like doing more than moaning about the weather, and there's good reason for it – it's unpredictable, and rarely consistent.

An hour later at 2pm, Peter left home to go back to work, leaving Ann to relax for the afternoon. Half hour later, Sheila phoned Ann to discuss details of the party, the call didn't last long and Ann was free after to that to soak up the rays.

At around 3.30pm, a friend of Ann's passed by the house on a bus and saw her sunbathing in the large garden. There was seemingly nothing untoward and no sign of the danger to come. 45 minutes later, Ann was spotted driving her car by a lorry driver and his passenger.

They knew Ann through her daughter, Ann Marie, and when they saw her car, they beeped the horn and Ann waved back. They remembered seeing one man in the passenger seat and another in the back but had no idea who they were.

At 4.45pm, a passing motorist saw a blue car on the driveway of Ann's home, which didn't belong to her. A few minutes later but before 5pm, another witness saw a blue van with two men parked up at the end of the driveway to the house.

At 5pm, Ann was murdered by having her throat cut, and her bikini bottoms were removed. Five minutes later, a passing taxi driver saw a tanned man in thick trousers running away from the house, estimated to be in his thirties.

The driver also noticed a blue car speed down the driveway, screech into the road, and head towards Darlington town centre. At 6pm, peter returned home from work to find the front door open and made his way to the sunbed in the garden.

Beside the empty sunbed on a small table, the radio was still playing, and a cigarette was in the ashtray, along with a half-drunk glass of wine. Peter went back into the house and found Ann lying face down on the living room floor in a pool of blood.

Lack of evidence

Police arrived within minutes and kickstarted one of the biggest manhunts in County Durham's history. At first, due to the couple's mild wealth and luxury country house, robbery was put forward as the motive behind the attack, except the house hadn't been robbed.

Sexual assault was the next motive to look at but despite Ann's body missing her bikini bottoms, there were no signs of abuse. Two theories relate to the bikini bottoms, one was that due to the heat she was sunbathing partially nude or was wrapped in a towel, and the second was that her killer removed her bikini bottoms to make it look like she had been sexually assaulted when she hadn't been.

Ann had her throat cut with a very sharp blade that a coroner suspected may have been a razor, she had also been stabbed in the neck, either with the same blade or a different one. The attack had severed a major artery and Ann's blood soaked into the floor around her body, leading one officer to call it a bloodbath.

There were no signs of a struggle or forced entry, which meant that Ann most likely knew her killer, unless someone had approached her while she sunbathed in the garden, which meant the doors to the property would already have been open.

Unsurprisingly, the investigation looked to the then 55-year-old Peter as the main suspect. Detectives uncovered an affair between Peter and a younger barmaid at the Dinsdale Golf Club that he frequently visited, which would have given Peter motive to murder his wife.

It was also suspected at the same time that someone close to the barmaid may have found out about it and decided to punish Peter by killing Ann. However, in the days following the murder, Peter's colleagues confirmed that he was at work at the time of the murder, thus giving him a solid alibi.

He also didn't look like the person running away from the scene and refused a solicitor on the basis that he hadn't done anything wrong. He remarried three years later in 1993 in a private ceremony, but not to the barmaid he was having an affair with.

Despite the alibis, lack of forensic evidence against him, and no real motive, Peter was rearrested in 2005 and charged with Ann's murder. Durham Police's infatuation with Peter being the killer may have let the real killer get away with murder.

Coldest of the cold

Unsurprisingly, the case against Peter was dropped in the same year due to a lack of evidence, which meant Durham Police were clutching at straws. Peter's children and family claimed the case had been damaging to him and that Durham Police had failed to meet a good standard of policing which had compromised the quality of the investigation.

And not without just cause, for the police didn't look into the blue car until many years later, and other suspects were not considered at the time due to their fixation on Peter and trying to make the evidence fit him as the killer.

By the Spring of 1991, the case had gone cold, despite many press conferences in which Peter pleaded with the killer to come forward, and a Crimewatch UK reconstruction for TV. Then, in early 1993, a woman reported an unusual story to police.

She claimed that a man had walked into the card shop she was working at, and in conversation with her boss, boasted about killing Ann. The woman claimed that her boss had taken the man into the back room to discuss bulk purchases.

The boss came out of the stock room with a pale white face, as the man walked past him and out the front door. The boss relayed the story to her and said the man would never be caught as he was moving to Australia the next day. The man was never found.

In late 1994, The Northern Echo newspaper and Durham Police received multiple letters from a man claiming to be the killer. He wrote how much he enjoyed killing Ann and the rush he got from it. Though the source of the letters have never been traced, experts have debunked them as fiction.

Questioning witness reliability

Aside from the 2005 misstep that led to Peter's arrest, the last big update on the case came in 2020, when the then 85-year-old Peter hired a private investigator named Jen Jarvie. He concluded his investigation by saying that the killer may have been a violent criminal on the run from prison, a man named Michael Benson.

Benson was a convicted criminal with a history of robbery and assault, and one attack with a carving knife. During the summer of 1990, Benson was released from prison on licence but failed to report back and went on the run.

He also owned a blue car similar to the one seen in the driveway of the house. He was rearrested not long after and was never considered a suspect at the time, though he had been questioned about his whereabouts on that day. He died of natural causes in 2011.

Many oddities surround the case and the official timeline, with many questioning the reliability of the witnesses. The lorry driver who had seen Ann at 4.15pm, said he had beeped his horn and Ann waved back at him.

This meant, that according to other witnesses, Ann was sunbathing in her bikini at 3.30pm, driving around town fully clothed with two men 45 minutes later, and then back in a bikini an hour after that, near the time she was murdered.

It's possible the lorry driver didn't see Ann with two men and only thought he did. Driving a lorry on the hottest day of the year would have made it difficult to keep focus on everything. The driver's statement wasn't given until many weeks after the murder.

No obvious motive

At least two witnesses put a blue car near to the house or in the driveway at around the time Ann was murdered, which suggests that the driver of the blue car could have been the killer, or at least aware of what had happened.

It doesn't explain the man running away from the house, but he could have been someone else in the car who disagreed with what happened or a runner wearing jogging bottoms, getting as sweaty as he could under the hot sun. But the big question remained – what was the motive?

There were no signs of robbery or sexual assault, despite Ann missing her bikini bottoms, and no signs of forced entry. Ann wasn't tortured or stabbed multiple times in a frenzy, she had her throat cut and the killer walked away, pointing to the fact he might have been a thrill killer or someone involved in a pre-meditated hit.

Some researchers point to the barmaid as instigating a hit on Ann, to get her out the picture so she could be with Peter but there has been no evidence to prove it. As a barmaid, it was possible she spoke to all kinds of people in passing and may have mentioned her distaste for Ann.

She had the best of both worlds; Peter's sexual attention but without the responsibility of his children. It seems a strange kind of hit for Ann to have her throat cut, which would have ultimately led to further forensic evidence than a more professional hitman would have left.

Two more theories remain. One that the man who confessed in the card shop was indeed the killer.

Maybe he knew Ann and had made advances on her that were rejected. He drove to her house that day to convince her to be with him then killed her when she refused his advances.

The second was that the killing was opportunistic in nature which is why the killer has never been caught due to the randomness of it. While walking or driving past the house, the man – and it would have been a man – may have seen Ann sunbathing in the garden.

With the hot sun clouding his judgement, he perhaps took the violent decision to end her life. but again, this is mostly conjecture and theories. What we do know is that Ann Heron was killed for no apparent reason by an unidentified killer in a case that has never been solved. It remains County Durham's only unsolved murder of the 20th Century.

Charles Walton and the Quinton Witch

In 1945 Britain, witchcraft was long gone, but ask any local from the sleepy town of Lower Quinton, what happened to Charles Walton, and they'll tell you it was witchcraft!

Born in 1870, Charles Walton was a 74-year-old local gardener and hedge cutter who was brutally murdered on a cold Valentine's day in 1945. His body was found the same night on Firs Farm, on Meon Hill, Warwickshire. His death remains the oldest unsolved murder in Warwickshire.

Walton had been a landscaper and farm worker for most of his life, and despite walking with a stick, he was still able to take on minor jobs like hedge cutting. For nine months prior to his death, he had been working on Firs Farm, for the owner, Alfred Potter.

The day of the murder, Walton left home with his trusty pitchfork and a cutting hook and made his way to the farm. He was last seen walking past the local church at around nine in the morning. At some point during the day, Walton was brutally murdered.

Murder most horrid

Walton was living with his niece at the time of his death, Edith Walton, and she noticed he hadn't returned home at his usual time of 4pm. Due to his tendency to end up in the local pub, she dismissed it and visited her neighbour instead. By 6pm, when Walton hadn't returned, Edith and the neighbour walked over to Firs Farm and informed Alfred Potter.

Potter claimed he had last seen Walton cutting the hedges near the Hillground side of the farm, far away from the main farmhouse. The three of them traipsed over to where Walton had last been seen and stumbled upon a horrific sight.

Beside a hedgerow, hidden from view from the local lanes, was the body of Charles Walton. He had been beaten with his own stick and his neck had been cut open with the cutting hook. To top it off, the pitchfork had been driven through his neck, pinning him to the ground, and the cutting hook was left embedded in the side of his neck. A cross had been carved on his chest.

Potter, who was the only one who wasn't screaming by that point, alerted a passing local man, who in turn called the police. As the darkness set in across the hills, word was getting around Lower Quinton that old man Walton had been killed by witches.

Suspects and rumours

Professor James Webster, of the West Midlands Forensic Laboratory, arrived at the scene, hours after the police, and just before midnight. He was brought in to ascertain exactly what had happened and how many people had been involved in the murder. While he took the body away to work on it, Alfred Potter became the prime suspect.

He told police that he had been drinking at lunchtime with another farmer and had seen Walton in the Hillground cutting hedges shortly after. Due to the location the body was found at and the length of hedge that was cut, it was ascertained that Walton had been killed at approximately 2pm. Potter hadn't gone back to check on Walton as he would always make his own way home at around 4pm. On this occasion there had been a cow stuck in a ditch that required Potter's attention and he claimed he never saw Walton after that.

Before things got out of hand in the town, the local police requested the assistance of the

Metropolitan Police, who were better equipped to deal with such evil. Along with witches, rumours were spreading of escaped Italian prisoners of war who were being held at a camp nearby.

Two days after the murder, Chief Inspector Robert Fabian and Detective Sergeant Albert Webb arrived in Lower Quinton. They immediately ordered a local officer to stick to Alfred Potter like glue and report back on every little thing he did.

An interpreter was sent to the Italian World War Two camp to see if the killer had come from there but reported back that every prisoner had been accounted for on the day of the murder. At the same time, Professor James Webster returned with his post-mortem results and claimed that it would have taken a man of quite some strength to have killed Walton alone.

Prime suspect

Being a farmer all his life, 40-year-old Potter would have been strong enough to overpower Walton and push the pitchfork through him. Three days after the murder, Potter was interviewed for a second time by the detectives from the Met. But already, his story wasn't matching up with the previous interview, in terms of the time he had been drinking and when he had seen Walton near the hedge.

The cow that Potter had attempted to get out of the ditch had been tested and was found to have drowned the day before the murder. The cow wasn't removed from the ditch, known as Doomsday Ditch, until 3.30pm on the 14th, approximately two hours after the murder. Potter was struggling to account for his time and Chief Inspector Fabian suspected him to be the killer.

On the 20th of February, the local officer watching Potter let slip that the forensics were taking fingerprints from the murder weapons. At which point, Potter said that he had touched the murder weapons when he first came across the body. He also strongly believed that one of the Italians had managed to escape the camp and kill Walton, calling them all the names under the Sun.

When another officer came by the farm and told them that Military Police had arrested one of the prisoners at the camp, Potter punched the air with joy and celebrated with his wife. Even though, the story of the arrest was nothing to do with the murder of Walton.

Despite the strangeness of Potter's character and version of events, no fingerprints were found on the murder weapon and he was ultimately never charged with the murder. Despite Chief Fabian being certain he was the killer, he also stated there was no evidence and no motive for Potter to have killed Walton and had mostly come across as a calm and civil man.

Enter – witchcraft!

Links to an even older murder

On a warm Autumn night in 1875, 79-year-old Ann Tennant was brutally murdered in the village of Long Compton, just fifteen miles from Lower Quinton. While returning from the shops with a loaf of bread, she passed a local farm, where a drunken local man named James Heywood was sitting.

Heywood was known to be of simple mind and a village outcast and Ann hurried past him. Another farmer nearby witnessed what happened next. Without warning, Heywood grabbed his pitchfork and attacked Ann with it. He stabbed her in the legs, head and neck, continuously stabbing her until he was restrained by the farmer and his workers.

Heywood was heard screaming that Ann was a witch, as she lay dying from her deep wounds.

He was sent to trial for murder and ultimately found not guilty on the grounds of insanity. He was sent to Broadmoor Criminal Lunatic Asylum, which still stands to this day. In an interview to discover his reasons for attacking her, he explained that Ann was one of at least 18 witches in the village and surrounding villages, and that he intended to murder every single one of them.

He refused to give the names of the other witches, in case they killed the investigators or other locals, for revealing their identity. He believed that witches had been in the village for hundreds of years and had kept their identities secret so they could live among us. He claimed to have discovered this news from a local priest, whose job it was to protect the villages.

The ghastly climax of a pagan rite

Nine years after the Walton murder, and still no closer to an arrest, the two detectives made the link between the killing of Ann Tenant and Walton. Despite being separated by 70 years, the two murders were remarkably similar. A closer inspection revealed that Tennant had a cutting hook embedded into her neck, the same as Walton.

The detectives discovered that the method of murder, using the cutting hook and pitchfork, was an Anglo-Saxon method of killing witches. At around the same time, the Met were provided with evidence and material that has since never been released to the public. Leading to further speculation of something mysterious going on in Lower Quinton.

Chief Inspector Fabian later left the investigation unsolved, stating they had done all they could for the local police. As the years went by, when asked about the case, he had one final message for anyone looking into it.

"I advise anybody who is tempted at any time to venture into Black Magic, witchcraft, Shamanism

– call it what you will – to remember Charles Walton and to think of his death, which was clearly the ghastly climax of a pagan rite. There is no stronger argument for keeping as far away as possible from the villains with their swords, incense and mumbo-jumbo. It is prudence on which your future peace of mind and even your life could depend." Chief Inspector Fabian, many years after the Walton murder.

The Quinton Witch

What happened to Chief Inspector Fabian to have him leave the investigation? What material did he and his colleagues uncover? Did they discover evidence of a witch in the small English village? Over the years, many investigations have taken place and many theories have been put forward, all backed up with tons of supposed evidence, but the most common one is the following.

Charles Walton's great-grandparents were Thomas Walton and Ann Smith. Smith was Ann Tennant's maiden name, born in 1794. She gave birth to William Walton who was Charles Walton's grandfather. When Thomas died of illness five years later, she remarried John Tennant in 1819. This led some to believe that Ann Tennant was the great-grandmother of Charles Walton.

What does this have to do with Charles' murder? An old book about folklore written by a local priest had been sent to Chief Inspector Fabian from another officer. In it, there is a story regarding Charles Walton. In 1885, a young plough boy named Charles Walton was walking home from work at a farm when he encountered a ghostly black dog. This happened for three nights in a row until the last night when the dog was accompanied by a headless woman. On the last night, Walton's sister mysteriously died.

To the locals this was proof that Charles Walton was a witch and was even feared by some villagers. It was one of the reasons why he kept himself to himself. Locals later claimed he could cast evil spells and kept toads as pets, which were used to kill farmers crops. He was even said to have been involved in the death of Potter's cow, the night before his death.

Locals banded together and murdered Walton using an ancient ritual so that his blood could soak into the ground to replenish the land. Shortly after Walton was murdered, locals reported seeing black dogs on the field and on the lanes around the village.

If Charles Winton was a witch, then it stands to some bizarre reason that his great-grandmother was too. And so, if James Heywood is to be believed that there were 18 witches in the Warwickshire villages at the time of Ann's death, then Charles would have been the second. Only 16 witches to go.

Despite the tales of witchcraft, what we do know is that Charles Walton was murdered in a ritualistic fashion in a small English village, and the case has never been solved.

The MI6 Catfishing Case

A teenager created multiple online identities to trick his friend into believing he had been recruited by an MI6 agent to kill him, thereby setting up his own murder, in a bizarre tale of catfishing.

Most of us are familiar with the term 'catfish' and it's usually associated with someone using a fake identity to lure someone into a relationship or for financial benefit. In the MI6 Catfishing Case, a teenager was convinced to kill by the very person he was going to murder. Stay with me!

In Manchester, England, in 2003, a 16-year-old boy known only as Mark, due to his age, became besotted by a housewife named Janet Dobinson on an internet chatroom. She described herself as a woman in her forties, who unbeknownst to her husband, was actually an agent and spy for MI6.

Over many months, Mark became obsessed with Janet and their online relationship grew to the point that Janet had begun to trust Mark could keep secrets. She explained that if he could pass some MI6 initiation tests, that he could become a powerful MI6 asset and spy.

She told Mark that if he passed one final test then he would be paid £30,000 (GBP), taken to visit the queen and take part in a meeting with the then prime minister, Tony Blair. The final test was to be a secret bodyguard to a VIP named James Bell, who knew the code to a large safe at the bottom of the Atlantic Ocean, that if opened, could end the monarchy.

Coincidentally, James Bell lived only three miles away from Mark, and more coincidentally happened to be Mark's friend, 14-year-old John. Unknown to Mark, Janet was a fake online identity of John's, who was planning for his own friend to murder him for MI6 – but it wasn't the only fake identity.

Multiple crimes

Mark was using an MSN chatroom dedicated to Manchester teens, when he was messaged by a 16-year-old girl named Rachel, who he took a fancy to. Unbeknownst to Mark, the 16-year-old girl was also John. In fact, John had created six different identities to converse with Mark.

Rachel had given Mark a fake photo and tried to 'meet' with him on multiple occasions but made excuses for not showing up each time. She (John) created someone called Kevin who ended up chatting with Mark.

Kevin was Rachel's stalker, and in February 2003, Kevin 'kidnapped' Rachel and held her hostage. If Mark wanted her back then he needed to masturbate on live webcam for him. Mark followed Kevin's orders so he could rescue someone he had never met.

A few days later, Kevin said Rachel had been kidnapped again and gangraped before Kevin murdered her. Mark was introduced to Rachel's little brother, John – the real John who chatted to Mark as himself.

With no-one else to turn too over his grief, both John and Mark became friends and met in real life, to 'comfort' each other over the death of John's fake sister. Suddenly, Rachel returned to chat, claiming she had been in coma and had given birth to a baby and that it was Mark's.

Having not met in person, Mark denied it. Weeks later, Mark received a post-dated message from Rachel who claimed she was only trying to protect both Mark and John, and that if he had received this message then she was already dead somewhere.

Janet Dobinson

It wasn't until John created Janet that things began to get out of hand. Unsurprisingly, Janet knew all of John's movements and relayed them back to Mark, who became even more convinced that Janet had a huge amount of inside knowledge, and that it was information only known to someone who must have been a spy. Of course, it was John detailing his own movements.

Janet said that Manchester was a hub of British and foreign intelligence and that everyone from the hairdresser to the ice cream man was involved in some way. Janet was priming Mark to be one of the best spies in the city but she still needed proof he was willing to accept the deal.

The first test was to go to John's school and take him out of class for the day. Mark convinced his teacher's that John had an urgent appointment and both of them left to spend the day together, with Mark unaware that John was Janet.

Janet came up with various tasks including one mission that apparently had come direct from Tony Blair himself. She explained that James Bell had to be made to look gay. Mark would have to have oral sex with John so the hidden spies and enemies around Manchester would acknowledge it.

Unwilling to go through with it, Mark initially went against the idea but was convinced by Janet that it was for Queen and country, and of vital national security. Mark met John and went back to John's house where they performed oral sex on each other.

Attempted murder

On 29th June 2003, Mark was convinced to kill John as a matter of national security. Mark typed; *U want me 2 take him 2 trafford (sic) centre and kill him in the middle of trafford centre??* The reply was simple and forceful from Janet; *yes*. Mark agreed to kill his friend.

When Mark plunged the knife into 14-year-old John in Goose Green alley, in Altrincham town, he said, '*I love you bro*'. John later told detectives that Mark lifted him to his feet and stabbed him again, as he cried out for an ambulance, believing himself to be dying. Mark was said to have responded with; '*people will hear, please be quiet.*'

Less than 24 hours later, John was fighting for his life in hospital after being stabbed multiple times, in what police assumed to have been a robbery gone wrong. Little did they realise that a web of deceit had been spun so large that John had planned his own murder.

When police reviewed the CCTV footage following John through Manchester to Altrincham town centre, they watched Mark and John disappear down Goose Green alley where John was found. 25 minutes later, Mark left the alleyway alone and called police, claiming that a hooded man had attacked them.

The next day, the media, informed by police, put out an appeal looking for a hooded man in his early 20s, wearing black jeans, nothing like what Mark looked like. But Mark was already in custody, and due to his age, the police didn't update the press.

Mark pleaded guilty to attempted murder but claimed he was working for MI6. Even more bizarrely, John was charged with inciting his own murder, a charge so rare it had never been heard in a British court before.

Addicted to an illusion

When interviewed in his hospital bed, John claimed he had no idea why Mark had attacked him. John had been close to death and Mark might have been up on a murder charge, but John survived stab wounds to his kidney, liver, and gall bladder which had to be removed.

At first, police thought the story that Mark told of Janet and MI6 to be absurd until they brought in criminal intelligence analyst Sally Hogg to comb through both boy's computers. She analysed almost 60,000 lines of text generated between the two computers, which took her six weeks.

John had found Mark to be gullible and felt that using the multiple identities was like taking drugs. He had become addicted to tricking Mark and created a multi-layered story within the identities, which the judge in the trial later stated that, *'skilled writers of fiction would struggle to conjure up a plot such as that which arises here.'*

John had become so addicted to the illusion that he skipped meals and stayed at his laptop, simply needing to be on the internet to crave his chatroom hit. He went through many sleepless nights and typed the equivalent of 20 novels in his messages to Mark. The amount of data found on both computers relating to the chatroom equated to 133 gigabytes.

People who witnessed the trial were taken aback that a 14-year-old boy had created a *'matrix of deceit'*, manoeuvring an unsuspecting older boy into a web of deception, that some likened to brainwashing.

So why did a 14-year-old boy end up planning his own murder? The truth is rather more tragic than pretending he was a multi-billionaire who knew the code to a chest full of wealth so large that it could overthrow the British monarchy.

Alternate reality

It appeared that John was the victim of his own criminality. Psychologists stated that he hadn't arranged his death out of wickedness but out of fear. John had created an alternate reality for himself, built on various identities that he brought into his own reality.

The mission of the characters was to keep Mark in constant contact with John. Sally Hogg, the intelligence analyst said that each style of conversation for the identities were so distinct that even she believed some of them were different people. She claimed that the continuity and memory of each identity was nothing less than phenomenal.

John had a juvenile fascination with Mark that some considered to be love. In his own bizarre way, he was able to connect to Mark on a personal level and control him by using various made-up characters. The web of weirdness was so large that police had dedicated an entire room with coloured charts to work out exactly what had gone down.

Police later stated that MSN themselves should have been held responsible as there was no supervision available in the Manchester teen chatroom, and anyone could pose as whomever they liked. Back in 2003, internet anonymity was easier to pull off than it is today, and many privacy laws in place today were non-existent in 2003.

John later told a therapist that he wanted to be dead because after bringing his identities into his reality he felt as though he had no identity for himself and found himself lost in a veil of lies and bizarreness. Who better, John thought, than the love of his life to kill him on a mission for his country?

A novelty

Unsurprisingly, John was diagnosed with various mental health disorders, after having grown up in a broken household and a childhood filled with depression. He was also bullied in school and was known to bottle up his emotions.

Had the case been a straight-forward stabbing, Mark would have been sentenced to many years in prison but due to the bizarreness of the case, he was sentenced to serve probation in the community. John, who had the unusual status of being the first person charged and convicted of inciting their own murder, was sentenced to the same punishment.

Both boys were not allowed to use the internet unless under full supervision from an adult and were not allowed to contact each other. The story of Mark and John remained mostly hidden from the British media until after the trials had taken place.

According to John's therapist, he turned straight and found himself a girlfriend but ended up creating a web of lies around his life. He told her he was stabbed because he had identified a serial killer on the loose in Manchester.

This is an unusual case of catfishing that is both tragic and insightful, not least into how depression can affect teenagers, but how much the internet plays a role in developing alternate identities under the false veil of anonymity.

This was a case of a tragic manipulation by a damaged boy who convinced his friend he needed to die. When the judge in the case asked what the charge was, the prosecutor responded with, *'incitement to murder, but it's a novelty as nobody's ever been charged with inciting his own murder.'*

The judge concluded the hearing with, *'bizarre.'*

Madness of the Eriksson Twins

Two Swedish sisters said to be experiencing a shared psychosis called folie à deux went on days of bizarre and dangerous behaviour in England before ultimately ending with murder.

Many identical twins are said to share a special psychic connection, with as many as one in five claiming it to be true. Identical twins often finish each other's sentences and think the same thoughts but this is more to do with shared experiences than psychic powers.

For Swedish born Ursula and Sabina, their shared experiences saw them act out bizarre and dangerous behaviour that turned deadly. Both sisters were born in Värmland County, Southern Sweden, in 1967 to a loving family. They had an older sister named Mona and older brother named Björn.

They grew up with no obvious mental health issues and had no run-ins with the law, they were for all intents and purposes, model citizens. In their early thirties, the twins left Sweden, Sabina moved to County Cork, Ireland, with her partner, and Ursula left for the United States.

On 15th May 2008, Ursula arrived at Sabina's home in Ireland and they both got into a fight with Sabina's partner. A day later, in the early hours of the 16th, the twins left Sabina's home under cover of darkness and caught the morning ferry to Liverpool, England.

They arrived at around 8.30am and went to a local police station to report that Sabina's children by her partner may be in danger. Three hours later, the twins caught a coach to London and then things started to get weird.

Motorway Cops

The coach pulled into Keele services on the M6 motorway for an unscheduled pitstop because the twins told the driver they were too ill to continue the journey. The driver waited for them but when they tried to reboard the coach a few minutes later, at 1pm, the driver became suspicious.

Both twins were clinging onto their bags tightly as if hiding something. The driver requested to search their bags before reboarding but they refused. Using his coaching experience, the driver decided not to let them back on the coach, a decision that in hindsight may have been wise.

Before leaving, he informed the manager of the services that the twins were acting suspicious. The manager watched them on CCTV feeds and noticed they were unusually fixated on their bags. Concerned about the safety of other customers, she informed security and called the police.

Police arrived and talked to the twins but left shortly after as they felt the twins were in no danger, not did their bags contain anything untoward, despite holding them as if they contained something dangerous or valuable.

When the police left, the twins walked out of the services, across the car park, and straight onto the busy M6. They walked into oncoming traffic and almost caused a pile-up before walking along the central reservation. When they tried to cross the other lanes, Sabina was hit full-on by a car.

At that very moment, a TV show called Motorway Cops was being filmed for the BBC, when the Highways Agency and Traffic Police were informed of an incident on the M6, near Keele.

The documentary crew tagged along with the police and found the twins sitting on the side of the motorway with the driver of the car nearby. While they were investigating what had happened, and without warning, Ursula pushed past the officers and ran into oncoming traffic.

Systematically running into traffic

Ursula ran into the side of a lorry travelling at 60mph and was caught beneath the wheels with her legs being crushed. Then, as Ursula was being helped, Sabina ran into oncoming traffic and was knocked down a second time by a car travelling at high-speed.

Perplexed at what was going on, police shut down one of the motorway lanes and slowed down traffic. What had caused the twins to systematically run into oncoming traffic and put their lives at risk? Despite her legs being crushed, Ursula tried to fight off police who were trying to help.

She shouted that the police were not real and were imposters trying to kidnap them and steal their organs. Sabina, who had been unconscious for 15 minutes, suddenly came too, jumped to her feet, and started screaming for the police to help them, even though the police were right there.

She punched an officer in the face, then yet again ran into oncoming traffic. Now the traffic had been slowed down, members of the public restrained her until she was put in the back of an ambulance.

The documentary crew filmed the entire episode of bizarre behaviour, not realising that one of the sisters was about to go on and commit cold-blooded murder. Ursula was flown to hospital by helicopter and remanded to a psychiatric hospital for three months.

Despite being hit twice with a car in a matter of minutes, Sabina was released from hospital into police custody less than five hours later. Three days later, a court released her after only a one-day sentence for attacking an officer and motorway trespass. At no point had she received a psychiatric evaluation, something that would come back to haunt everyone involved.

Knife and hammer

With nowhere to go and no apparent concern for Ursula's wellbeing, Sabina wandered the streets of Stoke-on-Trent, carrying her only possessions in a clear plastic bag. In the early evening, 54-year-old paramedic and former RAF Airman Glenn Hollinshead was walking his dog with friend Peter Molloy.

Sabina asked them for directions to the nearest hotel as she was lost, and despite Molloy's concerns over her behaviour, Glenn suggested he take her back to his house to relax before finding a place to stay. It was then she mentioned she was looking for her sister in a hospital somewhere.

At Glenn's house, Sabina relaxed and had drinks with him and Peter. She was constantly looking out the window, worried someone was following her, and when Glenn tried to spark up a cigarette, she snatched it out his mouth, claiming it to be poisoned.

Molloy left just before midnight and Glenn allowed Sabina to stay the night. The next day, Glenn phoned around to try and locate Sabina's sister but had no luck. While preparing dinner later that evening, Sabina took a kitchen knife and stabbed Glenn in the head five times. He stumbled out his front door and died immediately from his wound.

Neighbours phoned police and watched Sabina running from Glenn's house. Sabina was holding a hammer and continuously hitting herself over the head with it. A passing driver saw her, jumped out his car, and tried to stop her causing more damage.

She hit the driver with the hammer and knocked him unconscious. She then dodged paramedics and police, and jumped off a 12-metre high bridge at Heron Cross. Though she survived the fall, she suffered a fractured skull and broke both her legs. But the weirdness was not over yet.

Folie à deux

On 11th September 2008, Sabina was discharged in a wheelchair and charged with murder on the same day. Ursula was also released from hospital custody around the same time and sent back to

Sweden. She ultimately returned to America and lived a perfectly normal life as a member of the Sacred Heart Church in Belle Vue, Washington.

A year later, the murder trial began, and Sabina pleaded guilty to manslaughter with diminished responsibility. She never explained why she had killed Glenn, nor could explain the bizarre behaviour from her and her sister.

Psychiatrists agreed that Sabina was a secondary sufferer of a psychosis known as folie à deux, which is a syndrome where symptoms of a delusional belief or hallucinations are transmitted from one individual to another. They claimed that Ursula suffered from psychosis and had transmitted her irrational thought processes to her sister.

Sabina was also diagnosed with a mental health disorder that made her hear voices accompanied with delusions but had no hallucinations. Sabina was sentenced to five years in prison and was released two years later in 2011, despite Glenn's family placing blame at the feet of the system that allowed Sabina to walk free in the first place with no psychiatric evaluation.

Glenn was known to help people all the time and taking Sabina into his home was nothing unusual for the former serviceman. He was merely a good Samaritan who took in someone who didn't understand the world around her.

Mind control

When the story got out in the press, there were many theories beyond folie à deux and mental health issues. The twin's brother, Björn, gave an interview to a Swedish newspaper in which he claimed his sisters were being hunted by maniacs which is why they were acting weird.

His basis was the belief his sisters were not mentally ill, and he was seeking an alternate but logical answer. It was suggested that the twins were involved in drug smuggling and were being chased by gangs.

A conspiracy later emerged that Glenn had been killed by two weapons suggesting that Sabina was innocent and was running from someone who had found her staying at Glenn's.

The wildest theory is that both twins were the subject of a mind control project, which is how Sabina stood up after 15 minutes of unconsciousness and ran back into oncoming traffic. The theories remain just that as there is no evidence to back them up – but if it was a mind control project then the evidence would have been hidden.

The bizarre behaviour of the twins on the M6 was broadcast on the BBC just a few weeks before Sabina killed Glenn. It could be one of the clearest examples of mentally transmitted psychological illness; folie à deux. Or it could be something more nefarious, a secret that only the twins knew.

Reincarnation of Two Murdered Girls

A year after two sisters were killed in a hit-and-run, their parents gave birth to twin girls, and claimed they were the reincarnated souls of the sisters, in one of the most convincing cases of reincarnation.

The town of Hexham, in Northumberland, England, is known predominantly for its Anglo-Saxon history, the Hexham Abbey, and its proximity to Hadrian's wall, the former Roman boundary between Roman Britannia, and Caledonia (Scotland) in the North.

For modern mystery and true crime enthusiasts, Hexham is known for the murder of the Pollock sisters, and their alleged reincarnation as twin girls to the same parents. John Pollock was born in Bristol in 1920, and met the love of his life, Joanna Pollock, in the same area.

Both were devout Catholics, with Florence carrying on the work of God at the Salvation Army in the city. Their third child and first daughter, Joanna Pollock, was born in 1946, and shortly after they moved to Hexham.

Their second daughter, Jacqueline, was born in 1951. John and Florence were busy with their new grocery and milk delivery business they had created, and so the two girls were mostly raised by their maternal grandmother.

In May of 1957, Joanna, 11, and Jacqueline, 6, were walking to church with their friend, Anthony, 9, when a nearby car revved up and purposely sped towards them. It crashed into them, killing both girls instantly, and leaving Anthony fighting for his life, only to die in hospital the next day.

Grief

A hit-and-run is bad enough but this was no accident. The female driver, who has never been named, was a Hexham local, who had recently been forcibly separated from her own children. She swallowed a large amount of prescription drugs then got into her car.

She erratically drove around town with the sole intention of killing herself and any children, out of revenge for hers being taken away. Witnesses to the crash watched in horror as the three children, trapped by a wall, were thrown into the air like ragdolls.

The woman managed to drive to the next road over, when the impact of the crash stopped the engine. Nearby pedestrians held her until police arrived. She was ultimately admitted to a psychiatric hospital and there remains little information as to what happened to her.

Understandably, both John and Florence fell into a deep depression that showed no signs of improving. As they grieved, and national press jumped on the story, they shared details of the girl's lives.

Eerily, Joanna often claimed to her father that she would never grow up to be a lady, which was a chilling premonition of her death. Jacqueline had been born with a birthmark on her left wrist and had a scar above her right eye after an accident when she was three.

Less than a year later, Florence became pregnant again, and John became convinced they were about to give birth to twin girls, who would be the reincarnated souls of their dead daughters.

Reincarnation

Florence didn't agree with John's beliefs and the twin theory was debunked by their doctor who detected only one heartbeat. The doctor also said it was extremely unlikely they would give birth to twins as no-one in their family had twins, nor was there any medical sign Florence was to have any.

In October 1958, Florence gave birth to – twins. The two girls were named Gillian and Jennifer. Despite being identical twins, the girls had different birthmarks. To their shock, the Pollock's discovered that Jennifer had two birthmarks, one on her left wrist, and one above her right eye, matching the birthmark and scar of Jacqueline.

When the girls were three-months-old, the family moved to Whitley Bay, 30 miles east of Hexham, where John and Florence restarted their business. It was there, they began to notice unusual traits that mimicked the personalities of their dead daughters.

Florence was still angry at John, as she believed he had prayed for Joanna and Jacqueline to be reincarnated before the girls had been killed, and that Gillian and Jennifer were the result of his prayers to God, and belief in reincarnation.

When the girls were three, they were able to identify toys belonging to Joanna and Jacqueline and separated them. Gillian claimed ownership of the toys that had belonged to Joanna, and Jennifer kept the toys that had belonged to Jacqueline.

Creepily, they referred to the toys with the same names as the deceased girls used. They also knew which toys had come from 'Santa Claus' and which had been gifted to them by their parents.

The blood is coming out the eyes

When the twins were four, the family took a day trip to Hexham, which led to more surprises. Without having ever visited Hexham, the girls were able to point out landmarks, knew where the school was that Joanna and Jacqueline had attended, and knew their way to the swings in a public park, as if they had been there before.

Still unconvinced, Florence continued to reject John's belief that the twins were the reincarnated souls of their dead daughters. That was until she overheard the two girls talking about the murder of their dead sisters.

When the girls were four, Florence was standing outside their bedroom as they played a game. She watched Gillian holding Jennifer's head and heard her say; '*the blood is coming out of your eyes. That is where the car hit you*'.

The two girls were known to have recreated the car crash on numerous occasions, with details that their parents confirmed they had never mentioned. Gillian also seemed to know that the birthmark on Jennifer's head was in the same location where Jennifer hit her head aged three.

Whenever they were outside, the twins had a fear of cars, and when a car revved its engine, they would cling to each other in fear. Jennifer was once heard saying; '*the car is coming to get us and take us away.*'

Reincarnation researcher

At the same time that Florence started to believe that reincarnation was possible, a researcher named Ian Stevenson, who had read of the story in the newspapers, contacted the Pollocks to arrange a meeting with the twins.

Known for his research into reincarnation, Ian interviewed the parents and twins at great length, noting birthmarks, stories, and memories of the past. No findings were published initially but he met them again in 1967 and then in 1978 when the twins were twenty.

Blood tests taken in 1978 showed they were identical twins, which normally meant the birthmarks would be in the same place, but they weren't. After Florence's death in 1979, and John's in 1985, Ian published a detailed case report on the possibility of the twins reincarnation.

It detailed in great length how the twins talked about the car accident in the present tense, as if they reliving it each time. The report also detailed similarities in personality between the twins and the two deceased girls.

Ian was an unbiased researcher but was a researcher into reincarnation, nonetheless. He worked on 895 cases of reincarnation, with 14 cases closer to proof of reincarnation than any others. The Pollock sisters were included in that list of 14.

Yet even Ian concluded that any reincarnation evidence is likely linked to influences in childhood. Despite the Pollock twins begin touted as proof of reincarnation, many have argued against it, and claimed that John specifically had embedded that idea into his children.

Parental impression

Florence and John claimed they never spoke to the girls about their dead sisters until they were much older, but it's likely that the twins may have learnt the story of Joanna and Jacqueline through their older brothers.

It's also not uncommon for young children to pick up on the stresses of their parents, and as Florence and John were still grieving, it's likely they projected their grief onto the twins. They would also have been fearful of cars and talked about Hexham a lot before the visit there.

Later on in life, the adult twins simply accepted their parents beliefs they were the reincarnated souls of their sisters but were sceptical about the notion of reincarnation in general. They claimed to have no memory of any previous life.

Ian later claimed that the case was 'evidentially weak' due to the only witnesses being the parents, and the death of the girls being talked about by them and other relatives while the twins were growing up. A journalist later claimed that if

John had not believed in reincarnation, then there would have been nothing to report.

However, Ian later wrote that genetics could not explain Jennifer's birthmark and found it inconceivable that John or Florence could have moulded the twins behaviours to match that of their dead daughters.

Reincarnation or parental impression? Mystery or explainable? Wherever we lay on the spectrum, it remains difficult to imagine how psychologically damaging the murder of children is to the parents who experience it.

Whether the parents instilled their beliefs into the twins, or whether the twins were indeed the reincarnated souls of their sisters, comes down to your belief as to whether reincarnation exists, or not.

Smelly Bobby Tulip

Robert Black was convicted of four murders but has been linked to at least 21 more, making him one of Britain's most prolific serial killers, with an unusual and disturbing taste for young girls.

There have been many British serial killers but perhaps none more disturbed and horrific than the story of rapist and murderer Robert Black. Black was a paedophile and killer who operated from 1969 to 1987.

He was a truck driver who made regular work trips to mainland Europe where it is suspected he murdered dozens more, and as time has moved on, the links have become more certain.

He was also prime suspect in the infamous 1978 disappearance and murder of 13-year-old Genette Tate, who had vanished on her newspaper delivery round in Devon, on England's Southern Coast. Her murder remains unsolved but linked to Black.

Black was born in Grangemouth, Scotland, in 1947. As his mother didn't know who Robert's father was, she had him adopted soon after and he was taken in by a couple who lived in Kinlochleven, in the Scottish Highlands.

Black went through life with the surname of Tulip, which he took from his adopted parents. He was called 'Smelly Bobby Tulip' by school friends due to his poor hygiene – and the name stuck. When he was growing up, he became an outcast and was prone to outbursts of anger and aggression.

From an early age, Black believed he should have been born a girl, and at five-years-old was caught comparing his genitalia with a girl of the same age. From the age of eight, he would insert objects into his anus and was known to have carried on with the unusual practice into his adulthood.

Disturbed from a young age

Black was knowing to wet the bed on regular occasions, which has been linked as one of the many pre-cursors to violence in later life. Every time he did so, he was beaten by his foster mother and couldn't fight back, resulting in numerous marks and regular bruising on his body.

When he was 11, both his foster parents died from apparent natural causes, and he was adopted by another couple in the small village. In the same year, he dragged a younger girl into a public toilet and attempted to rape her.

Concerned by his violent and abusive behaviour, his new foster parents had him removed from their care to a mixed-sex children's care home near Falkirk on the central belt of Scotland. Straight away, Black tried to abuse some of the girls there and sent to a stricter care home for boys only.

While there, and for the next three years, he was abused himself by a male carer and would regularly be forced to perform oral sex on him. He was also bullied physical and sexually by the other boys despite requiring to be constantly isolated due to his behaviour.

In 1963, when he was 16, he left the care home on his own accord and more into a small flat. He became a delivery boy for a local butcher and manipulated the deliveries so that he could deliver to houses with young girls who were alone. He later claimed to have touched or attacked at least 30 young girls on his deliveries.

In the same year, he lured a seven-year-old girl to an abandoned air-raid shelter then throttled her until she passed out, before masturbating over her body. He was arrested but a psychiatrist's report claimed it was only a one-off and he was let go without punishment.

Black was only 16 at the time and had attempted rape multiple times, been raped himself, and sexually attacked over 30 girls. It should have been clear to psychiatrist's then that Black was an immense danger to society. As it was, he was left to evolve from an abuser to a killer.

First confirmed victim

In 1968, when he was 21, Black moved to London after being released from a borstal on another offence of child abuse. He moved to a bedsit near King's Cross Station where young children were in plentiful supply.

He had multiple jobs, including a life-guard position that he was fired from for sexually touching a young girl – which comes as no surprise in hindsight. He started collecting child pornography through a contact at an illegal book shop in King's Cross.

He later managed to get hold of VHS tapes depicting child abuse. He also covertly took photos of children at swimming pools and in shops and kept the images in locked suitcases, due to the amount of material he had amassed.

He then moved into the attic of a Scottish couple in the area and got himself a long-distance driving job. In his truck he kept various disguises including different types of glasses. He also alternated between having a long beard and no beard at all.

His first confirmed murder victim came when he was 34, in August of 1981. He abducted nine-year-old Jennifer Cardy in Northern Ireland, while on a long-haul journey. She had been riding her bike near to a main road when she vanished.

Hundreds of volunteers joined the search for the girl, and her body was found in a large lake, six days later by two fishermen. Black had brutally raped and drowned the girl. The police suspected the killer might have been a truck driver due to the location of the lake to the trunk road.

Even though it would have been someone who was familiar with the roads around it, no connection was made to Black and his past convictions. It seemed that Black was able to get away with abuse and murder so easily that he ended up incorporating it into his truck routes.

Multiple murders and connections

His second confirmed murder victim was 11-year-old Susan Claire Maxwell, from Cornhill-on-Tweed, close to the Scottish border. Maxwell had been playing sports with friends and walked home alone, before being kidnapped by Black.

300 officers and hundreds more volunteers were involved in the search and an investigation was made of every property in the area, along with a huge amount of open land. A month later, in August of the same year, her decomposed body

was found by a lorry driver in a shallow grave at the side of the road. She had been tied up and gagged, with her underwear carefully positioned under her head.

Another three confirmed victims turned up from 1983 to 1987. There were also multiple disappearances and murders that were later linked to Black. In the United Kingdom alone, six more disappearances and murders were attributed to him.

There were also disappearances and murders across Ireland, the Netherlands and Germany. All of the victims vanished or were killed at the same time as Black would have been in the areas on his long-haul European journeys.

A full victim list and linked victim list can be found after the bibliography at the back of this book.

Cutting grass

The nationwide manhunt for Robert Black was one of the most expensive and most resource-heavy UK murder investigations of the 20th century. But he was caught when a member of the public witnessed one of his abductions.

On 14th July 1990, 53-year-old retiree David Herkes was cutting his grass when he saw a blue van slow down on the other side of the road. Herkes started to clean the blades of his lawnmower and happened to look up to see the feet of a small girl lifted from the pavement and into the van.

He watched as Black pushed the girl into the passenger seat before quickly getting in and driving away. Already, Herkes believed he had witnessed an abduction and wrote down the registration number. He realised it might have been the six-year-old daughter of his neighbour and ran to her house where they called the police immediately.

Within minutes the area was covered in police vehicles. A short while passed and Herkes continued to describe what had happened to officers. Suddenly, Black had decided to drive back through the town on his way northwards and Herkes recognised the van instantly.

He shouted to officers who jumped in front of the van and pulled Black from his seat. The father of the missing girl charged into the van and found his daughter tied up in a sleeping bag. She had already been sexually abused but had survived and would go on to make a full recovery. It was the last child that Black would ever touch.

Prime suspect

In 1994, Black was convicted of the rape and murder of three girls, along with kidnapping and sexual assault. He received a sentence of life imprisonment with a minimum of 35 years. The case caused outrage in the United Kingdom and saw protests calling for the death penalty to be reinstated in the country.

Up until his death, he was charged with another murder from 1981 and was about to be charged with more when he died of a heart attack in January 2016. He was already a prime suspect in most of his suspected victims.

Robert Black remains one of the worst serial killers to walk the streets of the United Kingdom and Europe. Not only was his brutality unheard of in the British Isles at the time, but the huge number of lives he affected was never forgotten.

The unusual aspect of the Robert Black case is that many unsolved murders and disappearances of young girls across the United Kingdom and Europe in the 1980s and 1990s, continue to be linked to him.

Many feel that Black has become a catch-all name for many local police forces to use for 'solving' unsolved cases. Not unlike Henry Lee Lucas in the United States, when at one point in time, over 3,000 murders were attributed him, clearing the unsolved slate of many local law enforcement agencies.

Due to his extensive travelling and number of disappearance on his truck routes, it is possible that Black was one of the most prolific serial killers ever to walk the British Isles and Europe. But with his passing, Smell Bobby Tulip has taken his numerous secrets to the grave.

Mystery of the Body in the Tree

In 1940s England, a group of young boys were playing in the forest when they found a dead woman stuffed into the middle of a wych elm tree.

Hagley Wood on first sight is a beautiful English forest in Worcestershire, but it holds a macabre secret that has never been solved. In April 1943, while World War Two was still going on, four local boys, Robert Hart, Thomas Willetts, Bob Farmer and Fred Payne, ventured onto the private land of Lord Cobham, known as Hagley Estate.

They were out searching for birds' nests to steal their eggs, an old English pastime for kids with nothing else to do. While searching for the perfect location to begin their hunt, they ventured to Wychbury Hill and found themselves staring at a large dead wych elm tree. Believing it to be a perfect location for nesting birds, Farmer began climbing.

Pushed on by his friends, he got to the top of the trunk and looked down into the middle of the tree. There, at the bottom of the tree was a skull, which wasn't uncommon for forests in England, due to the proliferation of wildlife. However, the skull had hair. Curious, he reached down and lifted the skull out of the tree to show his friends.

On realising the skull had human teeth, they found the rest of the skeleton inside the tree. Suddenly they realised they were on private land and threw the skull back into the tree and ran away from the location. The boys returned home and decided not to tell anyone about what they had found. Except, Farmer felt uneasy about what he had found and eventually told his parents.

Investigation

The next morning, police descended onto Wychbury Hill and began their investigation. They found the near-complete skeletal remains of a female, along with various items of clothing and a gold wedding ring. When the area was searched, the bones of her missing hand were found a short distance away.

Forensic testing showed that the female had been dead for at least eighteen months and was suspected to have been suffocated to death, due to remnants of a cloth found in her mouth. The body would have been placed inside the tree at the time of her death, while it was still warm. Had it been subjected to rigor mortis then the body would not have fitted inside.

Due to the upheaval of the war, identification of the body became difficult. Too many people were being reported missing on a weekly, if not daily basis, for the police to cross reference each and every one of them. The investigation ground to a halt. Despite her dentistry being unique, there was no match forthcoming and her case went cold almost immediately. Until the graffiti began.

Meme before memes

One year after the discovery of the body and failure of the investigation, mysterious graffiti began appearing around the local area and then the whole of the country. The first of the graffiti was spotted in Birmingham, twelve miles away from Hagley Wood.

It read; *Who Put Bella In The Wych Elm*.

For some bizarre reason, the graffiti took hold and multiplied across the country, becoming synonymous with the body in the tree. It was clear that despite the case running cold, someone had not forgotten what happened to the person they called Bella.

The Bella graffiti continued appearing on walls, gravestones, and trees, and has never stopped appearing. Bella had become more famous in death than in life but still, her real identity had never been solved, and her suspect remained uncaptured.

Close to the summit of Wychbury Hill, just 150 metres from the West Midlands border, is a monument known as the Wychbury Obelisk, or Hagley Obelisk, visible for miles around. Every Spring, the same graffiti, written to be in the same handwriting style appears on the monument.

The theories

The name of Bella first appeared with the graffiti and had not been proposed by anyone before that. Had the killer created the first of the graffiti? Did someone know who the victim was and never came forward to identify her? These questions and more have haunted cold case investigators for years and have led to various theories about her death and her identity.

In 1941, a German spy named Josef Jakobs parachuted into England but injured himself on landing and was captured shortly after. He claimed that his lover, whom he had a photo of, had also just landed in England, after being trained as a spy, but no trace of her entering the country ever existed. In 2016, it was concluded that his lover, Clara Bauerle, had died in a German hospital around the same time.

In a 1944 Birmingham police report, a Brummie sex worker reported that another prostitute named Bella, which was short for Luebella, had disappeared at about the time the body in the tree was said to have been killed. The case was never followed up by police and the report is the only record of the missing prostitute named Bella.

Then of course – witchcraft!

In 1945, a London archaeologist, Margaret Murray, claimed that the death was a result of witchcraft. The hand that had been found away from the body had been cut off as part of a ritual. She believed the murder had been carried out by occult gypsies during a ritual called the Hand of Glory. The press at the time seemed to favour the story of witchcraft and ran with it for many years.

Many more theories emerged over the years, including one that the victim was a Dutch national who had been killed by a German spy-ring. Another that Lord Cobham had her killed at an occult party on his estate. And yet another bizarre theory that Bella hadn't been found dead but that she was growing inside of the tree, due to the hair on the skull.

What happened to Bella?

One of the most logical, yet more disregarded theories comes from Hagley itself, but ten years after the incident.

In 1953, a police report shows that local Hagley resident, Una Mossop, went to the police after her ex-husband, Jack Mossop, had confessed to the murder before the body was even found. Jack and a Dutchman named Van Ralt, had been out drinking one night when they met a woman in the Lyttelton Arms in Hagley. The three of them got drunk together and left the pub later in the evening.

As they were driving through the village, the woman had passed out. Unsure what to do, they took her to a hollow tree in the woods, placed her inside, and assumed she had woken up in the morning and gone home. He confessed to his family the week after but they didn't believe it, instead finding him to be crazy.

Jack was confined to a psychiatric institute shortly after. He claimed to have nightmares of a girl staring at him from within the forest and that the forest was alive. Unfortunately, he died long before the body was even found by Farmer and his friends.

It has long remained unclear why Una waited a decade to retell his story, or why she had kept it secret for so long. There are no psychiatric records available to ascertain whether Jack was indeed having nightmares of the girl in the forest. If he had, then his story could have been a version of the truth.

It may also stand to reason that the woman getting drunk in the pub with them, was a prostitute named Luebella who had been reported missing. Despite the story, it has long been debunked by those who favour tales of witchcraft.

We may never know what happened to Bella or who she really is but her story continues to persist to this day. In England, in 2018, there was a 75th anniversary event of Bella's discovery, three miles away from the elm tree. It included authors, filmmakers, paranormal investigators, and live Bella-themed music!

Curiously, Bella's skeleton and original autopsy report are missing and have never been found, only adding to the mystery of the body in the tree.

Visions of Murder

From a brutal murder in London to one of the most convincing cases of psychic mediumship in the history of true crime.

On a cold London night in February 1983, 25-year-old Jaqueline Poole was raped, beaten, and strangled to death. The barmaid from Ruislip was living alone at the time and was due at work the next day.

When her family failed to contact her, the father of her boyfriend visited the home and became concerned for her wellbeing. He managed to enter the property through the living room window and was met with the gruesome sight of Poole's lifeless and brutalised body.

The media latched onto the story and murder was splashed all over the local newspapers but not many details of the crime were released. Detectives wanted to keep the details of the crime secret so that it could aid in their investigation.

One day after the murder, a young woman by the name of Christine Holohan, who was studying to become a professional medium, had a vision. Aged 22, she dreamt of a young woman named Jackie Hunt, who had been murdered in the most horrific of ways.

The following morning, she went to the police and described her vision to them. The police were shocked because Christine had given them Jaqueline Poole's maiden name, which was Hunt, a detail that hadn't been released to the public.

Christine told police that Jaqueline called in sick to work and was later visited by a shady man who she let into her apartment. She had apparently known the man but didn't really like him. As the evening continued, the man became violent and attacked her, brutally killing her with his bare hands.

Now, if you're thinking this all sounds like gobbledegook, then you might be right. But Christine was able to describe the murder scene in such detail that the leading detective believed everything she said. It took 18 years for science to catch up with Christine's testimony, at last giving the DNA evidence needed to convict the killer.

Psychic Witness

She met with Detective Andrew Smith and Officer Tony Batters and recounted the story that the vision had shown her. Though few details were released at the time, Holohan was able to list over 100 distinct details of the crime scene, none of which had been made public and were only known to the investigatory team.

Though the body was found on the living room floor, the attack had started in the bathroom, where Jaqueline had been trying to lock herself in. Christine told them the attack had started in the bathroom, another detail that was never released to the public.

Christine described the number of cushions there were and their exact positions, along with how the furniture had been moved around. She described how Jaqueline had changed clothes multiple times during the day and which newspapers were dotted around the home. She could even tell them how much coffee had been left in the cups.

After her description of the crime scene and the details of the murder, the detectives turned to her description of the killer. After allowing Christine to enter a trance-like state, she began talking about the killer.

The murderer

Jaqueline's ex-husband was in jail at the time of the murder but she would visit him on a regular basis, the most recent being two weeks before her death. Christine claimed that the prison, she referred to in the British slang term of 'nick', was the connection to the killer. Both Jaqueline and her husband knew the killer and Christine referred to the mystery killer as the 'bird'.

In her trance, Christine relayed the following information. The killer was five-foot eight, dark skin, wavy hair, in his early Twenties. He had arm tattoos of a sword, snake, or rose, and was a Taurus, born in the months of April or May. She even went as far as giving a name to the killer; Tony. But Tony went by a nickname called 'Pokie'.

She claimed the killer worked as a painter or some other profession that required him to use a brush, and that he had robbed people's homes in the past. With regards to the theft of jewellery from Jaqueline's home, Christine gave them the number of 221.

The officers learned that a nearby road had house numbers going up to 221. When they searched the nearby park, they found a small rock formation that covered a hole, a perfect place to hide the goods, which were missing. It was suspected the killer had buried the jewellery then returned later to collect them.

Despite the clues that Holohan was able to provide the police, the killer wasn't found at the time, but his DNA was kept on record for such a time when it could be used. It turns out, the investigation had to wait 18 years for Christine to be proven right.

Time's up!

In 2001, Anthony Ruark was arrested for Jaqueline's murder. He was arrested for theft just one year earlier and his DNA had been secured as part of the arrest. When the DNA was checked against the database, it was a match for some of the skin that was found underneath Jaqueline's fingernails. The killer had been caught and his time on the run was up.

Police went back and matched Christine's details with Ruark. He was five-foot nine of mixed race, and was born in late April, a Taurus. He was 23-years-old at the time of the murder, had many tattoos all over his body, and was a part time plasterer. He made most of his money robbing houses and stealing cars. More importantly, Tony was short for Anthony, and his was known by the nickname; Pokie.

With DNA evidence secured, along with Christine's testimony from the original investigation, Ruark was convicted of Jaqueline's rape, robbery, and murder, and sentenced to life in prison.

The details that Christine had given the original investigation were considered so good that it remains one of the most convincing cases of psychic mediumship in the history of crime.

Killings of Templeton Woods

After the first Templeton Woods murder, girls stopped walking the streets alone, after the second, the area became ground zero for Britain's most infamous cold case, with links to the Zodiac Killer.

Located a short drive north of Dundee City Centre, in Scotland, Templeton Woods is considered a great place to visit for walking, cycling, horse riding, picnics, or to watch the wonderful wildlife that lives there. You might even spot a red squirrel or two!

Templeton Woods is a relatively small council wood, covering an area of just under 150 acres, dwarfed by some of Scotland's larger landscapes. Surprising then that the woods are known across the world, not as a place of beauty, but of murder.

From 1979 to 1987, three murders of young women took place in and near the woods, and although one of them appeared to be solved, the other two remain a mystery to this day.

Combined with reports of women being attacked there as recently as 2017, then perhaps it's no surprise why Templeton Woods is draped in such infamy and terror.

1979

As a schoolgirl, Carol Lannen didn't leave much of an impression on her peers at the time, she was a quiet girl who kept herself to herself and didn't have many friends to shout about. However, her death at the age of 18, did leave an impression.

On 21st March 1979, prostitute Carol got into a red estate car on Exchange Street in Dundee City and it was the last time anyone saw her alive – apart from her killer. The next day, her nude body was found near a picnic table in Templeton Woods. She had been tied up and strangled to death.

As the police investigation grew, other prostitutes were able to describe the driver of the red car to police. Over 6,000 owners of red cars were interviewed and an artist-sketch of the suspect, based on the witness accounts, was released to the public.

11 days later, her personal belongings and clothes were found on the side of River Don, over 70 miles away, north of Aberdeen. The murder of Carol Lannen changed the way teenage girls in Dundee conducted themselves, according to recent interviews of women who were teenagers at the time.

And like many crimes in the 1970s, the case went cold and the murder went unsolved, a dark footnote to cap off a year of change for the country. Until 1980, when a second murder in Templeton Woods rocked Dundee and the whole of Scotland.

1980

As a trainee nursery nurse, 20-year-old Elizabeth McCabe needed to let her hair down occasionally. In February 1980, she and a friend went out drinking in popular bars around Dundee. She left a nightclub in the early hours of 11th February – and never made it home.

She was reported missing by her family the same morning. Two weeks later, on the day of what would have been her 21st Birthday, Elizabeth's body was found by two rabbit hunters out walking their dogs, who initially thought they had unearthed a mannequin.

When police arrived, they found her partially nude body in the undergrowth. She had been strangled to death, just 150 metres away from where Carol's body was discovered 11 months earlier. When the newspapers got hold of it and linked it to the 1979 death, the *Templeton Woods Murders* were birthed into existence.

With the severe possibility that a serial attacker was loose in Dundee, the police launched what would become the largest murder investigation the region had ever seen. An estimated 7,500 people were interviewed, and the records of every accommodation owner in the city were scoured for clues.

But as in the death of Carol Lannen, the case went cold – until 2005. Using new forensic techniques, former taxi driver Vincent Simpson was arrested and charged with Elizabeth's murder, based on the evidence that his DNA was found on a blue jumper near the body – which may or may not have had anything to do with the murder.

Unsurprisingly, after a seven-week trial, the jury found Simpson not guilty. The police admitted the evidence had been fundamentally flawed and potentially contaminated. However, the police were known to have fixated their efforts on taxi drivers in the city to such an extent that they took manpower away from other possibilities.

And so it was that Elizabeth McCabe's murder fell into the realm of the unsolved the same way Carol's had. But in 1987, a murder in nearby Melville Lower Wood, led to an altogether different suspect.

1987

30-year-old Lynda Hunter worked with the Samaritans and was a qualified social worker who disappeared on 21st August 1987. The next day, her husband, Andrew Hunter, officially reported her missing.

Immediately, due to his suspicious nature, Andrew became the suspect in her disappearance but the police needed more evidence – or a body – to charge him with anything. They began investigating his life and pulling the pieces apart.

Andrew was a voluntary worker at the Salvation Army, where he had met Lynda via the Samaritans, and they had an affair while he was still married. In December 1984, his wife, Christine, died of suicide, found hanging by a noose in the attic of her home.

During his relationship with Lynda, he took a gay lover and visited gay saunas in Glasgow and Edinburgh. He was also known to every prostitute in Dundee, becoming a regular client to many, and to top it off, he had a 22-year-old drug addicted girlfriend on the side.

Seven months after her disappearance, Lynda's body was found in Melville Lower Wood, in Ladybank, Fife, just 18 miles from Templeton Woods. She had been strangled with her dog lead. Police swooped in on Andrew Hunter and arrested him for her murder.

Despite pleading his innocence, Andrew was charged and ultimately convicted of Lynda's murder in 1988. Andrew had killed her because she became pregnant and he dumped her body in the woods to hide the evidence. Just five years later, in 1993, Andrew died of a heart attack while in prison.

But some suggest he had taken many secrets to the grave.

Enter the sleuths

Hunter's case had gained considerable interest across the entire United Kingdom, as it was the first Scottish case to be shown on the national Crimewatch program in 1987. Because of that, Andrew was linked to the Templeton Woods murders, not least because of his regular visits to Dundee.

The description of the driver given to police by witnesses in the Carol Lannen case seemed to be a strikingly close fit to that of Hunter. He was also known to have abused his wife, and Lynda, along with having a penchant for walks through local woods and fetishized sex.

While many have linked him with the Templeton Woods murders, he never gave any inclination he was involved, and any supposed evidence against him has washed away with time.

Interestingly, the authorities have closed the cases and have no new plans to reopen them but it hasn't stopped an army of online sleuths and researchers attempting to solve them. So, who was responsible for the Templeton Woods murders?

World's End murders

In October 1977, 18 months before Carol Lannen's death, two 17-year-old girls were murdered on different nights in Edinburgh, 60 miles from Dundee. They were both last seen leaving the World's End Pub in the city's old town. Their killer was Angus Sinclair.

He had previously killed his eight-year-old neighbour in 1961, for which he served 10 years inside. In 1982, he pleaded guilty to the rape and assault of 11 children aged six to 14 and was sentenced to life in prison.

In 2001, he was first charged with the World's End murders, but after various controversies with botched forensics, he was acquitted. An amendment to the double jeopardy law later saw him convicted of the murders in 2014, along with the 1978 murder of 17-year-old Mary Gallacher in Glasgow.

Then, he was linked to four other young women killed in Scotland between 1977 and 1978, leading to some suspecting he was the Templeton Woods murderer. But police records show that Sinclair was in custody for a firearms charge at the time of both women's deaths.

However, many prisoners were allowed out on work release, with much of the work release program going unrecorded in the late 1970s.

Partner in crime

Sinclair was so certain about the similarities between the murders that he feared being charged with both Templeton Woods deaths, due to the circumstantial evidence. Carol's purse and clothing were found on the riverbank near Aberdeen, a city where Sinclair was working in a motel before his firearm arrest – and after.

The photofit was a close match to his appearance, and the fact he had been convicted of four murders and multiple rapes, led some to believe he was the killer. But if Sinclair was in custody at the time, and had not been given work release – which is unrecorded – then who killed them?

Sinclair was known to have a partner in crime, named Gordon Hamilton, who helped him lure his victims, and also killed on his own. Could it be that the Templeton Woods deaths were copycat killings, designed to look like the World's End murders, to cover Sinclair's tracks?

Whatever further secrets Sinclair had, died with him in 2019, while serving his sentence.

Zodiac Killer

For many, the Zodiac Killer is one of the most infamous cold cases in America, if not the world. Between December 1968 and October 1969, in San Francisco, five people were killed by an unidentified serial killer.

The killer gave himself the moniker of Zodiac by sending taunting letters to local newspapers, many of which contained strange ciphers and codes. In one of the letters, the killer claimed to have murdered 37 victims.

After the last known murder, the Zodiac Killer disappeared and theories about what happened to him have perpetuated online. Other murders across the world have been connected to the Zodiac Killer, including sprees in Italy, Germany, and for some – Scotland.

In 2009, Tayside Major Crimes Investigations received a dossier that had been researched by an unidentified author, claiming that the Zodiac Killer had left California for Scotland in the mid-1970s, and that he was still living in the country.

Zodiac's last act

The conveniently unknown author claimed to have identified an American man living in the north-east of Scotland as the prime suspect in the Zodiac killings. According to the author's research, the man was responsible for Carol's death, and suspected in Elizabeth's.

In 2015, the author sent an email to a Scottish newspaper, and with regards to Carol's murder, claimed, *'this criminal act is often referred to as the first of 'The Templeton Woods Murders' my research formed a case study, which I submitted to Tayside CID in October 2009.'*

'As a result, an investigation was carried out into the suspect. Although stood down after six months, the suspect remains, to this day, 'under review'. There was no sex on the agenda, and it appears that empowerment was the motive. This I believe, was Zodiac's last act and had a different motive to the crimes in California.'

Though the Templeton Woods murder cases are seen as closed, authorities continue to log any new information that comes in. The killings could have been carried out by the Zodiac Killer, Angus Sinclair's partner, or an unidentified local man.

Perhaps the murders of Carol and Elizabeth were unconnected and it was merely a coincidence they were found so close together. Their deaths remain unsolved, and their killer or killers unidentified. Though it doesn't stop bizarre theories continuing to be talked about.

Templeton Woods continues to haunt investigators and true crime fans, as it has done for the past 40 years. It is one of Scotland's most infamous cold cases, and as time ticks on, the window for solving it gets ever smaller.

Look for more in the Orrible British True Crime Series!

OUT NOW!

For bibliographies, citations, true crime blog posts, more true crime books, and more information on new releases for your collection, head on over to www.benoakley.co.uk

Printed in Great Britain
by Amazon